THE TIME-LIFE ENCYCLOPEDIA OF GARDENING

Roses

by
JAMES UNDERWOOD CROCKETT
and
the Editors of TIME-LIFE BOOKS

Watercolor Illustrations by
Allianora Rosse

TIME-LIFE BOOKS, NEW YORK

THE AUTHOR: James Underwood Crockett is an eminent horticulturist and writer on gardening subjects. A graduate of the University of Massachusetts' Stockbridge School of Agriculture, he has lived in—and cultivated a wide variety of plants in—California, New York, Texas and New England and has served as a consultant to many nurseries and landscapers. His monthly bulletin, "Flowery Talks," is distributed to more than a million customers annually through florists' shops. Mr. Crockett lives in Massachusetts.

THE ILLUSTRATOR: Allianora Rosse, who provided the delicate, precise watercolors of rose varieties beginning on page 106, is a specialist in flower painting. Trained at the Art Academy of The Hague in The Netherlands, Miss Rosse worked for 16 years as staff artist for *Flower Grower* magazine. Her paintings and drawings of shrubs, trees and flowers have appeared in many books on gardening. Miss Rosse lives in New York City.

GENERAL CONSULTANTS: Peter Malins, Rosarian, Brooklyn Botanic Garden, New York City; Herbert C. Swim, Ontario, California; Joseph J. Kern, Euclid, Ohio.

THE COVER: A modern hybrid rose, the Lady Bird Johnson, is the spectacular result of an amateur rose breeder's success. The variety was introduced in 1970 after six years of experimentation by Eldon Curtis, a Dallas insurance man and rose hobbyist *(page 93)*.

TIME-LIFE BOOKS

EDITOR
Jerry Korn
EXECUTIVE EDITOR
A. B. C. Whipple
PLANNING
Oliver E. Allen
TEXT DIRECTOR
Martin Mann
ART DIRECTOR
Sheldon Cotler
CHIEF OF RESEARCH
Beatrice T. Dobie
PICTURE EDITOR
Robert G. Mason

Assistant Text Directors: Ogden Tanner, Diana Hirsh
Assistant Art Director: Arnold C. Holeywell
Assistant Chief of Research: Martha T. Goolrick
Assistant Picture Editor: Melvin L. Scott

PUBLISHER
Joan D. Manley
General Manager: John D. McSweeney
Business Manager: John Steven Maxwell
Sales Director: Carl G. Jaeger
Promotion Director: Beatrice K. Tolleris
Public Relations Director: Nicholas Benton

THE TIME-LIFE ENCYCLOPEDIA OF GARDENING

SERIES EDITOR: Robert M. Jones
EDITORIAL STAFF FOR ROSES:
Assistant Editor: Marian Gordon Goldman
Picture Editor: Adrian Condon
Designer: Leonard Wolfe
Staff Writers: Lee Greene, Suzanne Seixas, Gerald Simons, Peter Wood
Chief Researcher: Joan Mebane
Researchers: Evelyn Constable, Margo Dryden, Helen Fennell, Villette Harris, David Harrison, Susan Jonas, Gail Mattox
Design Assistant: Mervyn Clay
Staff Illustrator: Vincent Lewis

EDITORIAL PRODUCTION
Production Editor: Douglas B. Graham
Quality Director: Robert L. Young
Assistant: James J. Cox
Copy Staff: Rosalind Stubenberg, Heidi Sanford, Patricia Miller, Florence Keith
Picture Department: Dolores A. Littles, Barbara S. Simon

Valuable assistance was provided by the following individuals and departments of Time Inc.: Editorial Production, Robert W. Boyd Jr., Margaret T. Fischer; Editorial Reference, Peter Draz; Picture Collection, Doris O'Neil; Photographic Laboratory, George Karas; TIME-LIFE News Service, Murray J. Gart; Correspondent Holland McCombs (Dallas).

CONTENTS

The queen of flowers 1

Sooner or later, everyone who has a garden thinks about growing roses. There are practical reasons—if a gardener needs them—for deciding to do just that. For one thing, roses outperform practically every other kind of garden plant in the number of flowers they produce, in the length of their blooming season and in their normal life expectancy. But most gardeners become rose growers simply because they fall in love with the flowers. Roses have an irresistible combination of elegance and charm, thorny strength and satin-petaled delicacy, and their blooms come forth in a wonderful variety of colors, sizes, shapes and fragrances. It is this, the sensuous appeal of roses, that has made them the world's best-known and most popular ornamental plant.

Some people become so attached to roses that they talk to them, as if they were pets. Every once in a while I catch myself muttering words of encouragement to a plant that is slow to leaf out or begin blooming. I don't really believe that this helps the plant in any way, of course, but I must admit that it makes me feel better.

Any book about roses should open with words of encouragement to the beginner, who has perhaps been overwhelmed by the thought that roses make such unique demands on a gardener that growing them may be beyond his ability. Roses do require a certain amount of pampering. Yet it should be reassuring to remember that roses were growing long before there were human hands to tend to their needs. Fossil roses, found in rock formations in Colorado and Oregon, proved that wild roses date back 40 million years. They apparently originated in central Asia and spread all over the northern hemisphere, but inexplicably never crossed the equator—no truly wild roses have been discovered in the southern hemisphere. Almost everywhere else, however, wild roses can be found growing, often under difficult conditions—in the arctic cold of Alaska and Siberia, in the heat of India and North Africa. Wild roses grow in every state, and without much doubt there are some close to your home wherever you live. They thrive in the sand dunes

The Katherine T. Marshall, seen at left in bud and bloom, epitomizes the most popular class of rose, the hybrid tea, whose many-petaled blossoms come in a panoply of colors and reach 4 and more inches across.

7

of New England, in the wooded hills of New York, Indiana and Pennsylvania, in the open prairies of Missouri and Iowa and along streams in California.

Not all roses that are now called wild, however, are wild in the sense that they live on today untended in forests and fields. Many modern types are the results of long cultivation in ancient gardens and are more accurately termed species roses. They have become such independently distinct types that botanists consider them genetically established species, unlike most garden roses, which are genetically mixed hybrids.

The strangest thing about most truly wild roses is that their flowers do not look like roses at all. Instead of the familiar garden plant's bright globes, made up of large numbers of tightly interleaved petals, most wild rosebushes bear flowers that look like apple blossoms—one layer of five petals, a "single" in the horticulturist's term. This open form may help wild roses continue to survive without human care, since it exposes pollen for easy transmission by insects and wind, increasing the chances that the plant will reproduce in forests and fields.

Historical records indicate that wild roses were brought under cultivation in China about 5,000 years ago. By the time of the Han dynasties just before the Christian Era, rose gardens had become so popular that huge parks were devoted to them. It is said that land needed for agriculture was tied up, threatening food production and forcing the Emperor to order the destruction of some of the rose parks and to curtail rose culture in others. During this same period the Egyptians did a thriving business growing roses for the Romans, and according to some authorities shipped cut flowers to Rome via galley (how the flowers could be kept fresh for the long trip across the Mediterranean remains a mystery). The Romans were so enamored of roses that they also supported large nurseries in the south of Italy, particularly at Paestum (near the present-day city of Salerno); one order from the Emperor Nero for cut flowers for a night's feast reportedly ran up a bill totaling, in terms of modern currency, about $100,000.

After classical days, the "Queen of Flowers," as the Greeks described the rose, became less valued for its beauty than for its supposed medicinal value. Extracts were made from the dried petals and used in medicines and ointments for all sorts of ailments, though the only good they probably did was to disguise the taste of unpalatable concoctions. Roses for such purposes were produced by monasteries and private growers all over Europe, but the most famous center of culture was at Provins, outside Paris, which maintained its pre-eminence for six centuries—at one point the town's main street was lined with apothecary shops.

All these ancient roses and their descendants are in botanical terms members of a single group, or genus, *Rosa,* that is part of a much larger family of shrubs, herbs and trees known as *Rosaceae.* The rose's close relatives include not only strawberries, raspberries and hawthorn, but such fruits as the peach, almond, apple and apricot. In spite of the superficial differences among them, there are traits that connect them, such as blossoms that generally have petals in sets of five. Many bear edible fruit, and the rose is no exception. After a blossom's petals drop off they leave behind a small, round, usually red "hip." It is the raw material for rose-hip jelly—an old-fashioned favorite in England and New England—and is also an excellent source of vitamin C. (Rose hips were made into syrup to supply vitamin C to children in Britain during World War II, when supplies of citrus fruit, the usual vitamin C foodstuff, were cut off.) The resemblances among the members of the *Rosaceae* family have led some botanists to believe that all were descended from some prehistoric common ancestor, though its identity remains an unsolved mystery.

The ancestors of modern garden roses are easier to trace. The large number of varieties now in existence are, at least in part, descended from eight species of roses that began arriving in Europe from Asia around 1700. These roses entered into modern hybrids

GENEALOGY OF A QUEEN

The complex ancestry of the first and the most famous grandiflora rose, the Queen Elizabeth (pictured on page 119), reveals the multiple crossings that go into the creation of a modern hybrid rose. This chart names only the Queen's more recent ancestors, with their dates of introduction, types and colors. In an attempt to produce a new and more vigorous red rose, Dr. Walter E. Lammerts, a professional plant breeder in California, crossed one of his previous prize winners, the Charlotte Armstrong, with the Floradora, from quite a different lineage. After several tries that produced reddish roses with one defect or another, Dr. Lammerts grew a perfect one—in a glorious pink.

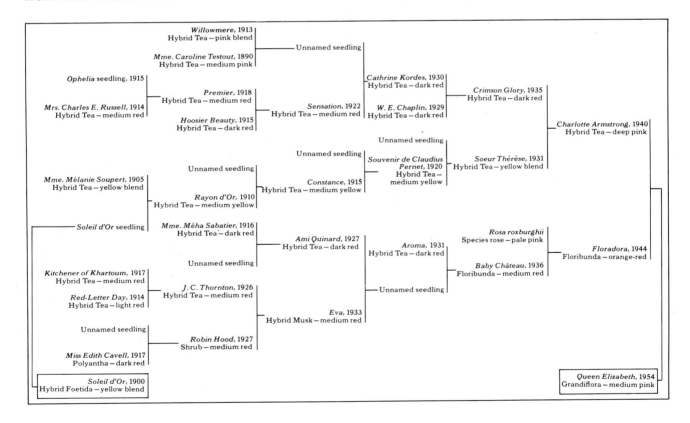

Willowmere, 1913
Hybrid Tea—pink blend

Mme. Caroline Testout, 1890
Hybrid Tea—medium pink

Unnamed seedling

Ophelia seedling, 1915

Mrs. Charles E. Russell, 1914
Hybrid Tea—medium red

Premier, 1918
Hybrid Tea—medium red

Hoosier Beauty, 1915
Hybrid Tea—dark red

Cathrine Kordes, 1930
Hybrid Tea—dark red

Crimson Glory, 1935
Hybrid Tea—dark red

Sensation, 1922
Hybrid Tea—medium red

W. E. Chaplin, 1929
Hybrid Tea—dark red

Unnamed seedling

Unnamed seedling

Souvenir de Claudius Pernet, 1920
Hybrid Tea—medium yellow

Soeur Thérèse, 1931
Hybrid Tea—yellow blend

Charlotte Armstrong, 1940
Hybrid Tea—deep pink

Mme. Mélanie Soupert, 1905
Hybrid Tea—yellow blend

Constance, 1915
Hybrid Tea—medium yellow

Rayon d'Or, 1910
Hybrid Tea—medium yellow

Soleil d'Or seedling

Mme. Méha Sabatier, 1916
Hybrid Tea—dark red

Ami Quinard, 1927
Hybrid Tea—dark red

Aroma, 1931
Hybrid Tea—dark red

Rosa roxburghii
Species rose—pale pink

Baby Château, 1936
Floribunda—medium red

Floradora, 1944
Floribunda—orange-red

Kitchener of Khartoum, 1917
Hybrid Tea—medium red

Unnamed seedling

J. C. Thornton, 1926
Hybrid Tea—medium red

Unnamed seedling

Red-Letter Day, 1914
Hybrid Tea—light red

Eva, 1933
Hybrid Musk—medium red

Unnamed seedling

Robin Hood, 1927
Shrub—medium red

Miss Edith Cavell, 1917
Polyantha—dark red

Soleil d'Or, 1900
Hybrid Foetida—yellow blend

Queen Elizabeth, 1954
Grandiflora—medium pink

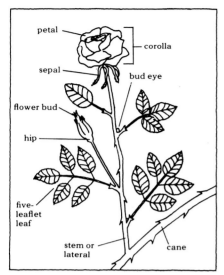

From its winter hiatus the rose in spring changes swiftly into a leafy, blooming plant. The bare canes first send out stems called laterals. Along these sprout the rose's distinctive teardrop-shaped leaflets in clusters—each cluster, which may have one, three, five, seven or nine leaflets, is botanically a single leaf. The stem completes its growth when it forms at its tip a tightly shut bud, or calyx, wrapped in leaflike sepals that curl away as the bud opens into a full blossom called a corolla. Normally, the blossom at the tip of the stem is the first to open. Other blossoms emerge lower down from tiny green "bud eyes," which appear at the bases of those leaflets having three or more leaflets.

principally because they possess a feature not commonly found in other roses: an ability to blossom repeatedly throughout the growing season—in some cases all season long—whereas most of the other species blossom just once in June or July. With this valuable attribute, however, some of the Asiatic roses, particularly the tea rose, *R. odorata,* and the China or Bengal rose, *R. chinensis,* carried a less desirable trait: a lack of hardiness. Not only are these two species native to a warm climate and thus inherently tender, but they have a tendency to continue to grow throughout the year. They persist in growing even in the face of frosts, unlike northern plants, which become dormant. They fight dormancy and die, whereas shrubs native to the north simply rest during the cold period of the year. Modern crossbreeding has produced hardy, cold-resistant hybrids from these delicate plants, and today their best qualities can be enjoyed in many areas *(Chapter 4 and map, page 153).*

Some of the best hybrids, however, turned out to have gained their hardiness at the cost of something else. Although they resisted cold, they were weak plants with spindly root systems, lacking in what horticulturists call vigor. The solution to this problem was discovered by pioneering rose growers, who joined the flower-bearing branches of weak but beautiful plants to the vigorous roots of wild roses, creating two plants in one. This practice is carried on today, no longer using roots collected from forests and hedgerows but exceptionally vigorous cultivated rootstocks such as selected forms of the *Rosa multiflora,* or Japanese rose; this grafting technique accounts for the knucklelike lump at the base of most rose plants—the so-called bud union where the root plant and the flowering plant have been joined together.

Toward the end of the 19th Century all except one of the elements of the modern rose had been supplied, but that missing characteristic was a trait longed for by rose growers—an attractive yellow color. There were yellow roses, but none were quite satisfactory. The ones among the recent Asiatic importations were a sulfurous rather than a pure yellow, and others among the wild or semiwild plants were inferior in size or shape.

The clue to the desired yellow turned up in the Parc de la Tête d'Or, the municipal gardens of Lyons, France. Strolling among its rosebushes one summer day in 1885, rose breeder Joseph Pernet-Ducher was struck by the golden shades of a Persian Yellow. Its flowers did not have the desired tea-rose shape, but its genetic traits, Pernet-Ducher decided, could introduce bright yellow into flowers of the hybrid-tea class.

His research took 25 years. After 13 years of crossbreeding he managed to create a still-popular rose, Soleil d'Or, that is light yellow on the outside but orange-red or pink inside. Twelve more years of crossing and back-crossing were necessary before he achieved the first pure yellow garden rose the world had ever seen: Rayon d'Or. From these and related varieties have come all the modern yellow, orange and flame-colored roses.

The value of a discovery such as a new color is so great—royalties may bring the grower millions of dollars—that rose breeding is always surrounded by an aura of romance and adventure. In 1939, when Francis Meilland found a sturdy plant with magnificent pale gold blossoms growing from one seed he had nurtured, he knew he had bred something valuable, but he had no idea how valuable—nor did he realize how long it would take him to find out. He sent cuttings to Germany, Italy and the United States—the bundle of stems addressed to a Pennsylvania rose grower was abroad the last American plane that got out of France in November 1940, a step ahead of the invading Nazis.

Not until World War II ended five years later did Meilland learn that his exported cuttings had been used to propagate the rose that many experts consider the best ever developed, the variety known in the U.S. as Peace. Within a decade the Peace rose was blossoming on more than 30 million bushes throughout the world. "How strange to think," Meilland said, "that all these millions of rosebushes sprang from a tiny seed no bigger than the head of a pin—a seed we might so easily have overlooked or neglected in a moment of inattention, or which might have been relished as a tidbit by some hungry field mouse."

Happily, the crossing, recrossing and back-crossing of roses of the past has produced so many varieties—about 5,000 are now available—that the gardener can find numbers suited to every part of the country and to every use imaginable. There are roses for formal and informal plantings, for landscaping effects and for ensuring privacy, for keeping the garden bright with color and for keeping the home liberally stocked with cut flowers. It is the gardener's pleasant task to choose the roses that are best adapted to his needs and tastes.

Despite the large number of rose varieties that are now being grown, all can be divided into groups, some classified by type, others by use. The descriptive listing of roses in Chapter 4, which provides information on more than 300 varieties, separates them into nine groups. (The proper botanical term for a hybrid rose created by a rose breeder is "cultivar," but the word "variety" is commonly used, as it is throughout this book.)

By far the most popular today is the hybrid tea, a clearly established type, or class, that offers an exceptional range of color, fragrance, flower size and shape for bouquets and for bright display in

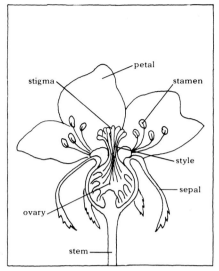

Cupped in the colorful petals of a rose are the reproductive organs that enable the plant to propagate itself from seed. Just inside the petals and their surrounding layer of leaflike sepals are stamens, the male organs, supporting round anthers. After the flower blooms, the anthers split to release pollen grains; these grains are blown by wind or picked up by insects and carried to a female organ, or pistil—in the same flower or in one that may be far away. The pistil is topped by a trumpet-shaped fuzzy cluster, the stigma; it catches pollen grains, which grow pollen tubes down through the slender column of the style to the ovary. There they fertilize the eggs and produce seeds.

THE FAMILIES OF ROSES

the garden. It turned up by chance in the gardens of a professional rose breeder, J. B. Guillot, near Lyons, France, in 1867. Guillot had planted seeds collected from a number of roses, and one of the seedlings surprised him with the beauty of its flower: a sweet, silvery pink rose he named La France. It is believed to be a descendant of the fragrant, bright pink, hybrid perpetual, Madame Victor Verdier, and the fragrant, creamy white tea rose, Madame Bravy—but neither Guillot nor anyone else could tell for certain. At the time of its introduction it was considered to be simply a particularly good hybrid perpetual, and not until 1880 did rose growers decide that it and similar new creations deserved a new class of their own, the hybrid tea.

Floribunda roses are products of the 20th Century, resulting from the mating of polyantha and hybrid tea roses, pioneered by D. T. Poulsen of Denmark, who worked to create a type that would thrive in northern Europe's severe climate. In 1924 Poulsen's son Sven introduced the first outstanding floribunda, the pink Else Poulsen. The floribunda lives up to the meaning of its Latin name, "flowers in abundance," for with ordinary care it will blossom without ceasing from early summer until frost. Floribunda colors cover the gamut of hues from snowy white to sparkling yellow to deep tones of crimson. No other rose is more adaptable to use in numerous garden settings, and no others, with the exception of shrub roses, thrive so well in combination with other kinds of plants.

Grandiflora roses, the product of crosses between hybrid teas and the free-flowering, sturdy floribunda roses, are generally a little taller and hardier than the hybrid teas, with a larger number of slightly smaller flowers. They were developed only recently, but such superb varieties as Queen Elizabeth have rapidly made them very popular.

Climbing roses are not a type of rose by themselves but a category of botanically diverse plants that have long arching or upright canes; many climbers, such as the hybrid tea climbers and the so-called large-flowered climbers, bear big blossoms, while others such as the ramblers and polyantha climbers, have small flowers. The climbers are misnamed in another sense, for no rose possesses tendrils that enable branches to attach themselves to a support; all must be tied to a trellis or wall or draped over it. But they have many uses, practical as well as esthetic. Left to grow as they please, they will clothe a naked embankment or soften the contours of a rocky outcropping. Trained to supports of various kinds, they will conceal an ugly foundation, follow a fence or wall, frame a doorway, climb high trellises and form thick screens in front of exposed patios and swimming pools. One special kind of climber, called a pillar rose, creates a spectacular effect; it has stiff canes that stand up nearly straight 8 feet or more and is usually grown tied to a post.

The rose known as polyantha, or occasionally as baby rambler, was created during the last quarter of the 19th Century by crossing dwarf forms of the China rose, *R. chinensis,* and the Japanese rose, *R. multiflora.* Today it has to a considerable degree been superseded by its own descendant, the floribunda. Yet polyanthas have many sterling qualities and are still widely grown, especially for massing in beds, for they are very hardy low-growing plants and bear large clusters of small flowers throughout the summer and fall. Polyanthas are widely grown by florists as pot plants for Easter and Mother's Day sales. Such plants may be set into the garden with every expectation that they will live and grow for many years. One I set out by a mailbox is still thriving after 18 years despite the dust of summer and the onslaught of snow-melting chemicals in the winter.

Like the polyanthas, the hybrid perpetual roses have lost out in favor of their offspring—in this case the hybrid teas. But the hybrid perpetuals, which also have tea roses among their ancestors, are tall, handsome, big-flowered plants, usually hardier than the hybrid teas. Their development in the early part of the 19th Century marked the end of an era. Those roses that preceded them are known as old roses, while hybrid perpetuals and others developed

HOW TO TIE UP A CLIMBER

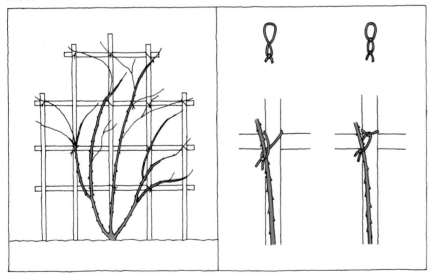

Because climbing roses lack the tendrils or "holdfasts" of true vines, they must be tied to a support such as a trellis, preferably in a fan shape. This arrangement stimulates more and better-distributed blossoms.

To tie a climber, loop string in a figure eight around the support and cane or stem before knotting (left). A more secure way is to tie the string around the support first, then again, loosely, around the stem (right).

since are called modern roses. They were tremendously popular for more than 50 years—in the 1880s one nurseryman alone listed over 800 varieties—for they combined huge and often intensely fragrant blossoms with hardiness, and many varieties bloomed repeatedly to provide flowers beyond the normal season. The name hybrid perpetual promises somewhat more than it delivers, however. Fully 90 per cent of the blossoms arrive at the first flush of bloom in early summer, and at that time hybrid perpetuals are the most colorful plants in the garden. Some varieties put forth a second, lighter display with the arrival of fall, and a few offer occasional flowers during the intervening period. Many gardeners today still prefer this schedule of flowering rather than the more regular production of hybrid teas.

The tea rose, *Rosa odorata,* originated countless years ago, probably from *R. chinensis,* the China, Bengal or monthly rose. Its climbing form derived from *R. odorata gigantea,* a climber from Burma and southwestern China that may grow 40 feet tall and bear blossoms 5 inches across. The varieties first brought to Europe from the Far East were double-flowering hybrids from gardens in the Orient, and they were given their name because many of them had a fragrance reminiscent of a newly emptied tea chest. Their colors range from white and blush to clear pink and various shades of yellow, including lemon, sulfur, apricot, buff, fawn and salmon. Tea roses bloom almost continuously and are slow to become dormant with the approach of cold weather. Thus they are easily killed by a sudden frost and are best suited to warm climates (Zones 8-10). Unlike hybrid teas, true tea roses grow well on their own roots and are often propagated from cuttings rather than from budding on other rootstalks.

For convenience, many other veterans of historic rose gardens are grouped in the general category of old roses, though in many cases they are unrelated or obscurely related, and some of them are newly bred additions to their types. Among the old roses are such plants as the pale alba rose; the moss rose, which secretes a substance that makes the buds sticky to touch but redolent of balsam; the cabbage or Provence rose, fragrant and many-petaled; the musk rose; the very ancient damask rose and the Noisette rose. Many of these have exotic flowers and a powerful fragrance, and their graceful, arching canes make an interesting contrast to the stiff, upright modern hybrids.

The ninth major grouping may be designated special-purpose roses. One such plant, the so-called tree rose, consists of almost any variety of rose plant grafted onto a tall main stem, or standard which usually requires a strong stake for support. The height of the upper plant determines how tall a tree rose will be; most are 2 to 5

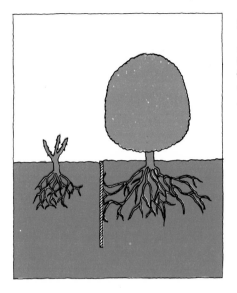

PROTECTING A ROSE'S ROOTS

Because roses are more vulnerable than most garden plants to competition from the invading roots of their neighbors, they need special protection when the plants are grown in front of shrubs or hedges such as privet, boxwood or yew—as they often are to show off their blossoms against a solid background of green. Before planting roses in a bed bordered by shrubs, excavate the bed and line the side toward the roses with a vertical shield of anodized aluminum or galvanized metal sheeting 18 to 24 inches wide, which can be purchased at some garden supply centers and at building supply or hardware stores.

feet tall, and, grown singly or in small groups in a prominent location, their effect is sensational. At the other end of the size scale is the miniature, or fairy, rose. The miniatures, many of them less than 1 foot high, are very hardy, continuously blooming rosebushes with perfect flowers about the size of a man's thumbnail. They serve very well in window boxes, rock gardens or in pots indoors.

Also included in this group are the shrub roses. For the most part they are species of wild roses, extremely hardy, vigorous and easy to maintain. A row of small shrub roses 3 or 4 feet tall makes an excellent garden boundary marker. While most shrub roses are handsome additions to any garden, a few species are too large for garden use. The multiflora, or Japanese, rose sends out such tall, dense, thorny growth that a hedgerow of the plants may reach 10 feet in height and 15 in thickness—but it will keep out any intruder larger than a rabbit.

Varied though the kinds of roses are, they are all members of one genus, with requirements for cultivation that set them apart from other plants. It is only natural for new gardeners to think that, because roses grow on bushes, they can grow under conditions that are suitable for other shrubs. But only some shrub roses are tough enough to grow with a minimum of soil preparation. Rosebushes' need for a certain amount of coddling comes from their unique hybrid background, since tender warm-climate plants are among their ancestors. Modern roses simply do not have the ability to grow as wild plants.

Another reason that roses need special attention is that they are extremely susceptible to root competition from other plants.

THE NEEDS OF ROSES

Tree roots are especially troublesome to roses, and when they are grown near trees, the tree roots must be sealed off from the rose bed with metal shields. Roses cannot compete well with many perennials, although some gardeners endeavor to combine the two types of plants in a border. To grow outstanding roses, plant them in a well-prepared bed by themselves.

The best place to grow roses is in full sunshine, for plants grown in the sun produce more flowers faster, and the bushes are apt to be sturdier. But almost any garden site that receives at least five to six hours of sunshine daily is suited for rose growing. Roses do not need sunshine all day long; a partially shaded area helps protect flower colors from fading. Early morning sun is to be preferred to afternoon sun, since it affords the plants an opportunity to dry off early in the day, thus cutting down on the incidence of leaf diseases common under moist conditions.

Good drainage is absolutely essential. Underground moisture, whether it comes from rain or conscientious watering, must not be allowed to accumulate at root level, for rose plants with "wet feet" can literally drown; roots need air as well as moisture. If a garden site that is otherwise acceptable lacks enough elevation to drain off naturally, its drainage can be improved by artificial means when the bed is prepared *(below)*. But the drainage of cold air is almost as important. Since cold air is heavier than warm air and will seek the lowest level, rose gardens should not be located in hollows. Many plants have died in frost pockets filled with stagnant cold air, while bushes only a few yards above them have come through without injury.

A garden site that is in the path of clearing breezes will be freed of dangerous frost pockets, but its plants may be heavily damaged by the breezes themselves, especially in winter. A moderate wind can quickly dry out exposed rose stems and whip long canes about, loosening the plants' roots. For these reasons, a good garden site will be open yet not fully exposed. Adequate windbreaks may be provided by a fence, a hedgerow or sturdy evergreens.

Finally, the gardener must make sure that his chosen garden site has the kind of soil that roses need to do their best. It has been said that any soil able to grow good corn will also grow good roses, but this is not a very helpful definition for suburbanites who have never grown corn.

The truth of the matter is that roses can be grown in almost any soil, but the soil may have to be modified. In some places—such as a few alkaline areas of the the West—the modification becomes extreme, requiring total replacement of existing soil to a depth of two feet. Almost everywhere, some minor adjustment of soil acidity is desirable, as is the addition of organic materials to improve soil texture, and fertilizer to add nutrients. Just how much modification your soil needs can be determined by testing it with a kit available at garden supply stores, or, for a more complete analysis, by sending a sample to the nearest office of your county agricultural extension service or a commercial soil-testing laboratory. Make no soil modification unless the test proves it necessary.

Roses do best in rather "heavy" soils—those that are mostly clay—to which an abundance of organic matter has been added to loosen the texture and help moisture drain away. If the soil is "light" —very sandy—even more organic matter should be added, for it prevents moisture from draining away too fast as well as too slowly. Of all the sources of organic matter, none suits roses more than well-rotted cow manure, but dried manure, ground peat moss or a compost made from decayed leaves will do. To help the plants grow strong roots, phosphorus compounds should also be mixed into the soil. Some gardeners use 20 per cent superphosphate, applied at the rate of 3 or 4 pounds per 100 square feet of garden area. Steamed bone meal is an alternative source of phosphorus, and may be applied at a rate of 3 to 6 pounds per 100 square feet. However, I prefer to use superphosphate since it gives you much more nourishment for your money.

Roses, like most garden plants, do best in soil that is very slightly acid—in terms of the numerical pH scale that is marked on the gauges of soil-testing kits, between 6.0 and 6.8 (7.0 is neutral and lower numbers indicate acidity, higher numbers alkalinity). For soils of average consistency, the pH can be raised 1 point —say, from 5.5 to 6.5—by adding 5 pounds of ground limestone per 100 square feet of garden area. To lower the pH ½ to 1 point, add 3 pounds of iron sulfate or ½ pound ground sulfur per 100 square feet.

None of these soil additives takes the place of the fertilizers that must be provided to nourish plants into vigorous bloom during the growing season *(Chapter 2)*. The additives are needed to prepare the bed for planting and they require some time to act on the soil. Therefore it is best to construct the bed several months before the actual planting will be done. In the North (Zones 3-5), where roses are usually planted in the spring, the bed should be prepared in the late fall, just before the ground freezes. In the more moderate climates of Zones 6 and 7, roses may be planted either in the late fall or early spring; if they are to be set out in the fall it is advisable to prepare the garden in midsummer. Preparation in early fall is advisable in the warm climates of Zones 8-10, where roses are generally planted when they are most nearly dormant—that is, in December, January or February.

The first step is to mark the outline of the bed. Of course its

BUILT-IN WATERING FOR DRY LOCATIONS

In hot, dry areas where roses require almost daily watering, a buried system saves work, and water, by getting moisture directly to the roots. Dig the bed to a depth of 2 feet and lay 2 inches of coarse gravel. Connect sections of 3- or 4-inch-diameter perforated composition pipe the length of the bed. Cap one end and extend the other, by using an elbow and unperforated sections, to ground level; this end, fitted with a strainer, is supplied with water from a hose. Cover the pipe with 2 inches of gravel and refill the bed.

BUILT-IN DRAINAGE FOR WET LOCATIONS

In damp areas—for example, where heavy clay soil retains so much water that rose plants may drown—a drain pipe under the bed will carry off excess water, provided it can empty at a lower level. Dig a trench 2 feet deep along the length of the rose bed and extend it to the downhill exit. Lay 2 inches of gravel in the trench, place 3- or 4-inch-diameter perforated pipe in position, and cover with another 2 inches of gravel before replacing the soil.

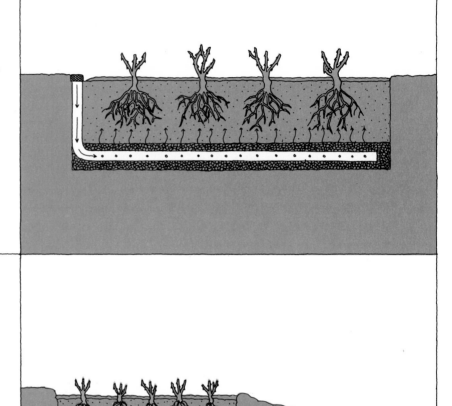

size and shape depend largely on the space available and personal taste but, unless the bed can be reached from two sides, it is wise to limit its width to no more than 5 feet. Then you can reach in among your plants to care for them properly, especially for spraying and dusting. If you want a wider bed, allow room for a footpath down the middle so you can reach all the plants easily.

Rose roots penetrate deeply into the soil, and for that reason it is necessary to prepare the soil much more deeply than one would for many other types of plants. I am of the opinion that one does not have to go to extremes in gardening and that it is not necessary to dig the soil to a depth of 4 feet, as was at one time advocated. Neither can you expect to have lovely roses if you simply scratch a hole in the ground and cram the roots into it. A well-prepared bed for roses should be excavated to a depth of 18 to 24 inches. Before digging, lay a tarpaulin, heavy paper or plastic on the grass beside the rose bed so that the soil can be piled on it. When the job is completed, the covering can be shaken free of soil, and the grass will still be clean. In digging the bed, first take off the sod and lay it to one side in a pile. Next, dig out the topsoil, which is darker in color than the subsoil beneath it, and pile it separately, and then remove as much subsoil as necessary.

PROVIDING SPECIAL DRAINAGE

At this point it is necessary to decide whether or not special drainage is required in order to keep water from standing in the bed during wet times of the year. If drainage must be provided from a sloping site, lay tile or composition drainage pipes in a trench from the bottom of the bed to a lower area. But there is no sense whatsoever in digging a bed in a wet area and putting in drains without having a lower area into which the water can flow; all you end up with is a sort of bathtub filled with water. When no such elevation differential exists, the only way to keep the soil well drained is to raise the rose bed above the general level of the soil around it. In parts of the Gulf Coast, for example, where there is a lot of rainfall and relatively level, poorly drained land, rose beds, as well as those of many other types of flowers, are normally elevated above the surrounding garden paths.

ENRICHING THE BED

Now comes the time to enrich the bed with the preparations previously discussed. First of all, if the garden site was formerly under grass, take the sods and lay them upside down on the bottom of the bed. The idea here, and in the operations that follow, is to get the surface materials, which are richer in organic content, down to the plants' roots, which will need all the nourishment they can get. Then the pile of topsoil is mixed with the organic additives—one third by volume—and spread evenly on top of the sods, and tamped down firmly but not compressed. Finally, the pile of subsoil is mixed with more organic additives, and with superphosphate or bone meal. When the enriched subsoil is replaced and tamped down, your new rose garden will be full to overflowing. But the bed will have at least three months in which to settle and mellow before the time for planting arrives.

HOW TO BUY ROSES

This long waiting period gives you plenty of time for the rose grower's off-season sport—poring over lists and catalogues to select the varieties that will be planted. The pictures of blossoms are always entrancing, but some very practical considerations should be kept in mind: winter hardiness (particularly in Zones 3-5), disease resistance, ease of maintenance, and plant size. These factors have all been taken into account in the annotated listings of Chapter 4. The varieties described are plants that I have found to be particularly noteworthy. Two other guides to good varieties are also helpful. One is provided by All-America Rose Selections, Incorporated, an association of rose growers and nurserymen which test-grows new varieties and endorses a few of the best; the AARS endorsement is marked on rose packages. The other guide is the rating provided by the American Rose Society, which grades rose varieties on a numerical scale. A rating of 10.0 would be perfect, and one variety, the silvery pink moss rose Jeanne de Montfort, came close to that ideal, scoring 9.9. However, any variety rated 8.0 or higher is a good choice (annual ratings for all varieties can be obtained at small cost by writing to the society at 4048 Roselea Place, Columbus, Ohio 43214).

There is a wide variation in the quality of individual rosebushes of the same type, of course. To assure yourself of the best plants, deal with a reputable seller and look on the package labels for the quality-grade markings established by the American Association of Nurserymen. The best plants of each variety are rated Number 1, while lesser plants are graded Number 1½ or Number 2. The roots and canes of Number 1 roses will be bigger, better developed and more numerous than those of lower-rated plants. (Specific factors considered in rating four groups of roses are shown

STANDARDS FOR ROSEBUSHES

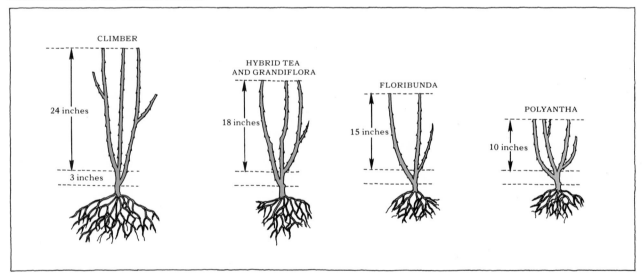

Rosebushes are graded 1, 1½ or 2, according to standards set for each of the types shown by the American Association of Nurserymen. To be rated No. 1, a hybrid tea, for example, must meet these requirements: when it is taken from the field it must be two years old and have three or more strong canes, two of which are 18 inches or longer, branching not higher than 3 inches above the knob of the bud union. The canes will not appear that long when the plant is bought because they will have been pruned to prevent breakage in handling and to keep the canes in balance with the root structure, some of which is cut off during the harvesting process.

in the illustration on page 20.) Since the price differential between a Number 1 and a Number 2 plant is not very great, I recommend that you ask for Number 1. The gardener who looks for bargains is likely to end up with a number of weak, undersized bushes. He may labor all summer to coax them along, but a Number 1½ or Number 2 bush will never equal a Number 1 in quantity or quality of flowers.

What the bushes look like when you actually buy them is determined by marketing practices. Rose plants are taken from the fields of the original growers when they are most nearly dormant and any remaining leaves can be removed (in some nurseries this chore used to be accomplished by letting a flock of sheep browse through the rose fields; now mechanical defoliators are used). At this point, the plant's bare roots are wrapped in moisture-preserving materials and the plants are put into protective packages for shipment to dealers and to mail-order buyers. The bare-root bushes must be planted before warm weather starts them growing again or they will die. Many dealers plant some bushes in pots to extend the selling season; potted bushes can be safely transplanted at any time, even while they are in full flower, and this makes them valuable as replacements for midseason casualties. But most rosebushes are sold in bare-root form and planted before the dormancy period ends in the spring.

Although planting time varies from place to place, you can buy your roses without undue worry about missing the local planting season. If you order in advance from a large mail-order house, even one in a distant state, your selection will be shipped to arrive at planting time in your area. If you prefer to wait until plants are available in local outlets and then buy in person, you will probably find a smaller selection, but in compensation the dealer has—and will share—valuable experience with rose-growing problems in your area.

Because most plants come concealed in their protective packages, you will probably see your roses for the first time when you unwrap them at home. You can tell at once if you bought high-quality plants. A good bush will have several plump, fresh, greenish canes; shriveled or discolored wood is usually a sign of dehydrated tissue. It will have several plump roots well distributed around the plant; the roots will be long and unbroken except perhaps for minor damage at one or two ends. Even the best bushes, however, will look rather strange to a beginning gardener. They are flowerless and leafless, with scraggly, sprawling roots, and it may seem highly unlikely that they will ever grow again. Yet from these unpromising bits of woody tissue will come blooms of unsurpassed beauty, and in only a few weeks.

ROSES THAT ARE NOT ROSES

Many plants having "rose" as part of their names are not related to the rose family at all, but are associated with it because of the shape or color of their blooms. The Christmas rose, for example, is an evergreen perennial whose white blossoms turn a roselike pink in winter. Rose mallow is another name for the stately hibiscus. Rose moss (not to be confused with the moss rose), is an annual of the portulaca genus with roselike flowers, and rose-of-heaven is a member of the pink family that boasts handsome, rose-colored flowers. Rose of Sharon, named after the Biblical plain, is actually a type of hibiscus with showy pink blossoms.

Royal families

Centuries of crossbreeding, accelerated by the development of scientific techniques in the 19th Century, have transformed the rosebushes of antiquity into a vast, interrelated lineage of flowers that today consists of many types, and numbers more than 13,000 identifiable varieties. The best-known and most popular of these are the hybrid tea roses, which account for virtually all of the cut roses sold by florists and for about three quarters of all roses produced commercially for gardens. Their popularity is understandable: they have long, pointed buds that open into large, symmetrical blossoms formed by the overlapping of many dozens of gracefully curving petals *(right)*. And in color they span the spectrum from white through every conceivable shade of pink, yellow and red to a maroon so deep as to appear almost black.

Between the sophisticated hybrid teas and their wild ancestors—some of which are still grown in gardens—are a host of other, less well-known roses. Among them is to be found virtually every characteristic that it is possible to breed into a flower. There are roses that stand erect, crawl along the ground, branch out to form magnificent hedges and cover entire walls. Some roses never grow more than a few inches high, while a few climbing varieties can reach 45 feet when tied to a fence or the side of a building for support. There are roses that produce dainty clusters of little flowers, each no bigger than a penny, and there are hybrid perpetuals that boast flowers as big as a man's face. Many roses have delightful fragrances reminiscent of tea, nuts, fruit, spices and honey, although there are a few that bring to mind the less pleasant aroma of stale beer or linseed oil. Others have completely lost their fragrances in the complicated breeding process that has also, surprisingly, produced some thornless roses.

Yet sweetly scented or odorless, large or small, prickly or smooth, delicately colored or dazzling in intensity, all roses share a common ancestral trait—a distinctive and memorable beauty that has earned for them the place of honor in the gardens of millions of flower lovers throughout the world.

In its unfolding petals, a hybrid tea rose displays the velvety texture, veining and rich color that make its type so popular.

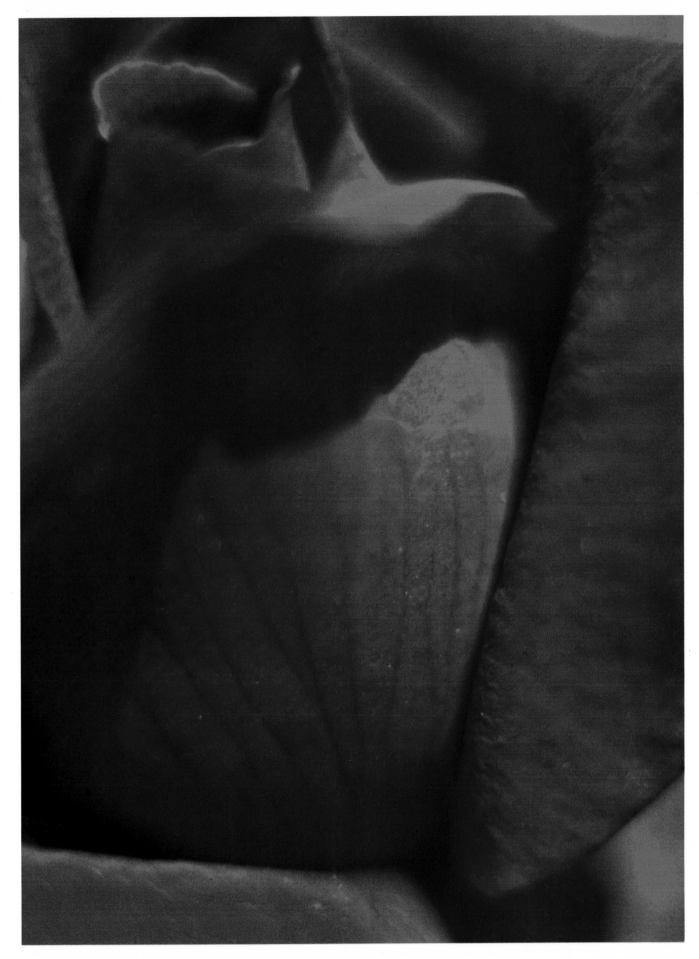

A bee's-eye view of a Rosa spinosissima hybrid called *Frühlingsgold* (*Spring Gold*) reveals a mass of pollen-tipped stamens.

The hardiest roses are the 200 or so wild or nearly wild varieties, called species roses, that are scattered around the world. Most of them are distinguished by their tall, shrublike growth and some are classified as shrub roses, others as climbers. They are usually easy to grow, and most bear five-petaled, intensely fragrant flowers that burst forth briefly each spring, occasionally repeating in the fall. While it is possible to transplant to home gardens some handsome varieties in their native state—*Rosa rugosa (below, left)* is an example—many wild roses are actually domesticated versions long cultivated in gardens, and some are man-made hybrids. By carefully matching types, breeders have been able to retain the charm of the wild rose while adding some wrinkles that nature never got around to, as in the golden version of *Rosa spinosissima (left)* and the long trailing variety known as Max Graf *(overleaf)*.

The reliable and hardy wild roses

A violet-hued Rosa rugosa rubra (above) grows wild near a sandy Nantucket beach. An unusually rugged variety of species rose that thrives in cool weather in almost any kind of soil, Rosa rugosa is often found growing near the seashore since it is one of the few plants not injured by salt spray.

The orange-yellow Rosa foetida bicolor (above, right), also known as Austrian Copper, has been called the most beautiful wild rose. A chance mutation of an all-yellow rose, it was originally brought to Europe before the 13th Century by the Moors who invaded Spain from Africa.

Clusters of pink blossoms adorn the long, flexible canes of Max Graf (right), a species hybrid that was created by crossing the tall, erect Rosa rugosa with the shorter, ground-hugging Rosa wichuraiana. The result is a long trailing rose that is widely used in landscape gardening (overleaf).

A hedgelike mass of Max Graf trailing roses, a species hybrid, provides a formal garden with a bushy border that sparkles

with delicate color. In addition to the species roses, the garden includes red and white climbers secured to pillars and trellises.

The king-sized hybrid perpetuals

Floral relics usually associated with Victorian England, where they achieved their greatest popularity, the hybrid perpetual roses are spectacularly large and full; the blooms of one variety, Paul Neyron, measure up to 7 inches in diameter and another, Prince Camille de Rohan, has blossoms with as many as 100 petals. The hybrid perpetuals (so named because they bloomed more frequently than earlier types) were the first of the modern hybrid roses, the result of many crossings and recrossings of various roses, especially those of the damask and China types. Although 19th Century rose growers eventually developed more than 3,000 varieties, the hybrid perpetuals were virtually eclipsed by the newer, more colorful and more regularly blooming hybrid tea roses after the turn of the century. But even today their superior cold resistance makes them a good choice for gardens in cool climates.

Pink and scarlet streaks mark a Ferdinand Pichard rose, one of the few hybrid perpetuals developed in this century. This variety grows 5 to 6 feet high, but is often pruned shorter and then trained to form a low, spreading bush.

A dramatic hybrid perpetual is J. B. Clark (right). It bears large, handsome flowers, and its canes grow so long—8 to 10 feet—that in some gardens they must be tied to vertical supports, like the canes of a climbing rose.

The prolific floribundas

The hardy floribunda roses, with their large, distinctive clusters of flowers, are the result of the crossing by a Danish rose breeder of the beautiful but relatively fragile hybrid tea rose with the sturdy polyantha, a dwarf rose noted for its dense bunches of tiny blossoms. Since then the floribundas have become second only to the hybrid teas in popularity among rose gardeners. Today hundreds of varieties fill gardens with great puffs of color all summer long, and are often used as informal hedges and as borders for sidewalks, walls and building foundations.

The five-petaled flowers of Betty Prior (above), a popular floribunda rose, closely resemble pink dogwood in shape, size and color, and have a pleasant, spicy fragrance. Like many older floribundas, this variety is usually grown as a shrub or as a hedge. It was introduced in 1938.

Europeana is one of the newer floribundas bred to provide handsome flowers suitable for cutting. A single cut stem can supply an instant bouquet of nearly two dozen large, brilliant red blossoms like those shown at right, each one containing as many as 25 to 30 ruffled petals.

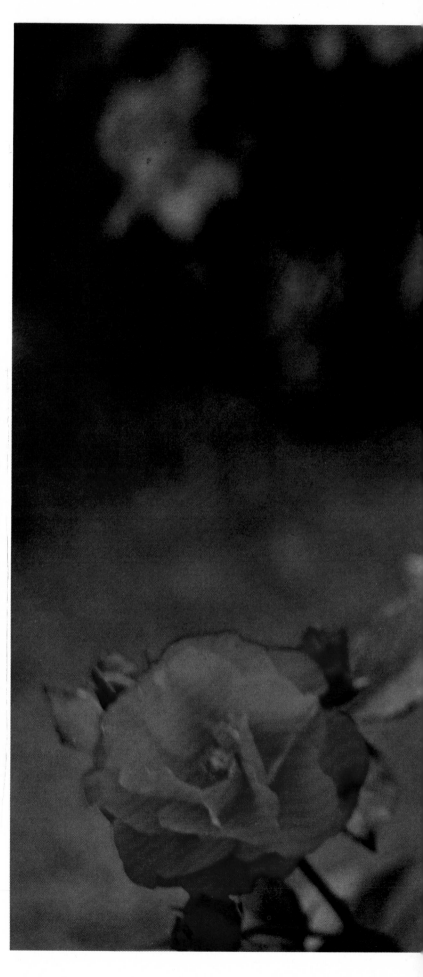

The stately grandifloras

One of the newest and most promising members of the rose family is the elegant grandiflora. A hybrid of hybrids, the grandiflora represents an ambitious attempt to create a novel type of rose that would have both the beautiful blossoms and long stems of the hybrid teas and the hardiness and flower clusters of the floribunda. While this goal has yet to be fully achieved, rose breeders have come tantalizingly close with the variety called Queen Elizabeth, shown at the left. Like most grandifloras, it grows quite high—it may reach 6 feet or more—and produces full-blossomed flowers, some singly and some in clusters. The flowers of most grandifloras are larger than those of floribundas, although not usually as large as those of the best hybrid teas. But when planted where its height can be shown to advantage, the grandiflora provides a more dramatic effect than either parent.

The Queen Elizabeth, named for Great Britain's Queen Elizabeth II, is considered by many rose growers to be the finest of the grandifloras. Bred from the hybrid tea Charlotte Armstrong and the floribunda Floradora, it is a remarkably vigorous and disease-free variety that bears small clusters of flowers on long, almost thornless stems.

33

The long-limbed climbers

Climbing roses are the acrobats of the rose family, plants whose canes grow so long that they can be trained to ascend trellises, posts and even rooftops or twine along fences and garden borders. Many types of roses can be used as climbers, including several varieties of floribundas, hybrid teas and wild roses.

The climbers with the largest spread are the ramblers, rugged plants that were a familiar sight in the United States around the turn of the century. Ramblers are extremely vigorous; it is not unusual for a young plant to grow 20 feet in a single season. In recent years ramblers have been largely replaced by climbers that are more manageable and have more spectacular blooms in a greater color range, particularly those varieties derived from hybrid teas *(below, left)* and floribundas *(bottom)*. Other climbers *(overleaf)* are the hybrids of wild roses.

The velvety bud of Don Juan (upper left) closely resembles that of another hybrid tea rose, New Yorker, from which it was bred. Like other moderate climbers, which grow up to 10 feet high, Don Juan can be used as a pillar rose when secured to a firm upright support.

Bloomfield Courage, a sturdy rambler rose whose canes sometimes grow 20 feet long, has a simple five-petaled flower (above) reminiscent of the old roses in its lineage. The aptly named ramblers extend canes in all directions and are often used to create a tall screen.

Bred from a tall, spreading variant of a standard-sized floribunda rose, Pillar of Fire is a climber that produces brilliant clusters of flowers 2 to 2½ inches in diameter. Floribunda climbers can be effective as informal hedges that provide privacy behind a wall of flowers.

A rustic effect was achieved by training a climbing rose, called Paul's Scarlet Climber, to grow along the top of a split-rail fence.

On Nantucket Island, where cottages covered with roses have become a tradition, hardy American Pillar climbing roses are tied to trellises running from the ground to the peak of the roof (above). These climbers will eventually cover the whole cottage with their bushy foliage.

Many climbing roses produce more blooms when trained laterally than when trained upward. At right the flower-covered canes of American Pillar roses stretch along a white picket fence in front of another seaside cottage in Nantucket that also has these climbers edging up its roof.

Dainty Bess is one of a small number of hybrid teas whose buds open into five-petaled blossoms like those of wild roses.

The favorites: hybrid teas

The development of the first hybrid tea rose in the mid-19th Century, a result of crossing the almost continuously blooming but fragile tea rose with the full-blossomed and vigorous hybrid perpetual *(pages 28-29)*, marked the beginning of a succession of notable triumphs in rose breeding. Over the last 50 years, the beautifully shaped, regularly blossoming flowers of the hybrid teas have come to dominate the rose gardens and florists' shops of the world. Today thousands of varieties are grown, and new ones are added every year. Their colors, shapes and sizes vary enormously, as shown by the sampling on these pages and overleaf, but all share a heritage of superlative beauty.

A hint of lavender in the pinkness of the hybrid tea rose Simone (above) marks a step in the attempt of rose breeders to introduce new shades— including gray and beige—into the colors of hybrid teas. The goal of more than one breeder is a blue rose.

The exquisite Tiffany rose (above, right) possesses the traits of an ideal hybrid tea: a memorable color (a blending of light pink and pale gold); long, pointed buds that open into large, high-centered flowers; and long stems suited for cutting and display.

Delicate shades of pink provide the distinctive coloration of the hybrid tea rose La Jolla (right). Bred from Charlotte Armstrong, an older hybrid tea that is the parent of many recent varieties, La Jolla opens into a full flower with as many as 45 petals.

A flawless bloom, the coral-tinted flower of the hybrid tea rose Hawaii, shown in a close-up at right, lends a touch of grandeur to

a garden in New Jersey. Seen in the beds in the background are the massed pinks of a grandiflora variety known as the Duet rose.

Planting, pruning and protection $\mathcal{2}$

Every experienced rose grower has his own little secrets for bringing a plant to the peak of free-flowering perfection. I have some pet methods of my own. But really there is no mysterious wizardry to rose culture. The techniques are simple, and if you apply them with some care, you will be rewarded with bumper crops of lovely blooms year after year.

The care begins at the beginning, with the planting of a new bush. This is done when the plant is dormant: in cold climates (Zones 3-5), in early spring; in moderate climates (Zones 6-7), in late fall or early spring; in warm climates (Zones 8-10), in the brief period of dormancy between December and February. But whenever planting time comes in your area, don't delay; plant the bushes as soon as possible after they arrive. And until you can get them into the ground, protect them carefully from drying out or freezing, or from sudden fluctuations in temperature.

When you receive your plants, remove their moisture-conserving wrappings immediately and dampen the roots. One way to keep them moist is to cover them with a wet piece of burlap; however, an even better way is to put the roots in a pail of water. This will enable the plants to absorb all of the moisture that their cells will hold. An old-fashioned, but excellent, trick is to use muddy water. If there is a considerable clay content in the mud, the roots will come out coated with a film of mud, which will keep them moist while they are being planted.

The plants may be left in the water up to 24 hours prior to planting if necessary. But rose roots must be protected from freezing as well as from dehydration, and care should be taken that bushes to be planted are not left out in the open overnight when freezing weather is expected. A combination of freezing temperatures and drying wind is especially lethal to roses. I once saw hundreds of healthy rose plants killed when careless nursery workers persisted in planting bare-root roses on a windy day when temperatures were only a few degrees below freezing. Even if the weather is mild, the

A large-flowered climber, of the variety named Peggy Ann Landon, showers a garden trellis with blooms. The full blossoming is the result of systematic pruning to remove dead wood and older, nonproductive canes.

PLANTING A BARE-ROOT ROSEBUSH

1. *If you cannot plant a bare-root rosebush immediately, protect it from drying out by "heeling in." Dig a slanting hole just deep enough so that you can cover the bush with soil. Then soak the heeled-in bush thoroughly.*

2. *Before planting a bare-root bush, fill a bucket with water and mix in a few handfuls of soil to help water adhere to the roots during planting. Soak the roots for at least two hours, making sure the knucklelike bud union is 3 to 4 inches below the water line.*

3. *Dig a hole about 18 inches deep, mix the soil you have removed with peat moss and fertilizer and replace most of the soil in a cone shape. Lay the roots over this cone so that the plant's bud union is level with the ground in Zones 6-7 (farther north it should be set an inch or so lower, farther south an inch or so higher). To gauge the height of the bud union, place a stick across the top of the hole.*

4. *Add more soil, covering the roots with 4 to 6 inches of soil. Then step into the hole and carefully firm the soil down with your feet.*

5. *Using a gentle flow from a hose, fill the hole until water begins to trickle over the sides. When the water has subsided, fill the hole to the top with additional soil.*

6. *To protect the plant from drying sun and wind until growth begins, build up a mound of soil around the bud union to a height of 8 inches, and water it periodically to keep it moist. For greater protection, surround each bush with a collar made from tar paper and filled with a moist mulch; the stakes driven inside the collar will keep it in place (inset).*

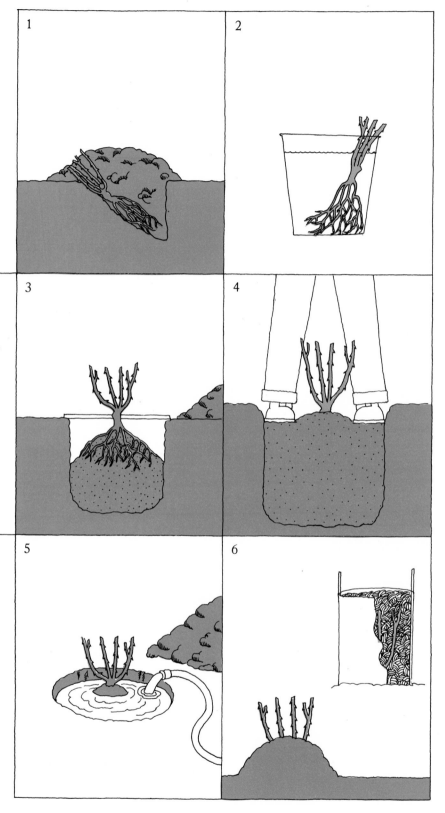

bushes should be carefully sheltered from desiccating winds. It is a good idea to put them, immersed in their pail of water, in a corner of an unheated garage where no wind at all can reach them.

If you cannot plant within a day or so, the bushes should be protected by a method known as heeling in. Very simply, a heeled-in plant is buried in a shallow ditch *(diagram, page 44)* that is slanted on the bottom. Place the roots at the deepest part and cover the whole plant, including the canes, with a thin layer of soil. If you have several plants to heel in, you can save labor by burying them close together in a single long, shallow trench. Keep the heeled-in plants well watered but not soggy.

Leave the plants with the roots protected and moist until you have dug holes for each in the prepared bed *(Chapter 1)*. There's a right way to dig holes, too. Spacing comes first, for rosebushes need room to spread. South of Zone 7, where the long, warm growing seasons make for exuberant growth, hybrid teas and similar bushes must be about 4 feet apart; in more northerly regions, the customary spacing is 3 feet. In every climate zone, the larger bushes—climbers, ramblers and shrub roses—should be 6 feet or more apart. To dig the hole itself, use a tapering, curve-bladed spade—its shape carves out neat cylindrical holes. Make the hole at least 18 inches wide and 18 inches deep to start; this is usually enough, but in some cases you may have to dig it out a bit more later to accommodate any of the roots that are unusually long.

Every plant has an optimum root depth that is set by the way the roots developed when the plant was first propagated. If the plant is transplanted to a considerably greater depth, the air supply that the roots need will be lessened by the deeper planting—they smother and die just as trees do when a lawn-grading operation piles dirt up too high around the trunks. The key to proper planting depth for most roses is the knucklelike knot of wood on the main stem, the bud union that appears on hybrid teas, floribundas, grandifloras and many climbers. It is at this point that an upper plant, chosen for its superior flowers, was joined to the understock of a species of wild rose having a big, rugged root system. When a bare-root bush is being planted, the bud union should be located at the garden's normal ground level if you live in a moderate climate (Zones 6-7). Northern gardeners (Zones 3-5) set their plants so that the bud union, which is very vulnerable to harm from cold, is located 1 to 2 inches below the surface. Southern gardeners (Zones 8-10), having little concern about cold weather, position the bud union about 1 to 2 inches above the surface, where sunlight stimulates a large

HEELING IN

HOW TO DIG THE HOLE

PLANTING DEPTH

number of canes to appear near the bud union, so that the plant becomes bushy faster.

To hold the plant with its bud union at the proper level, the hole must be adjusted to support the roots naturally. As you inspect a bare-root rose plant, you will notice that the roots fan out from the base of the main stem in a cone shape. To support the bush and retain the natural shape of the root system, fill in beneath the plant by mounding soil in the middle of the hole until the bud union is at the proper level.

At this point make sure the hole is big enough. Never cut back the roots of a rose plant so that the plant will fit into the hole that you have dug. If your plant has extremely long roots, or even one extremely long root, dig the hole big enough to accommodate the extra length without cramping. Do not make roots wind around the hole, but let them spread out in a natural manner. Just be thankful that your rose plant does have long roots that have not been cut off in the digging process. I should point out also that I do not believe in cutting off the tip of each rose root, a procedure that some experts recommend on the theory that it stimulates the growth of thin new "feeder" roots. In my opinion, all this trimming does is expose raw cells to infection from rot. Unless the ends of the roots are broken, split or badly bruised, or thick sections of the roots are broken, there is no reason whatsoever for making new cuts.

With the plant set to the desired level, fill in around it with soil. The usual practice is to fill in 4 to 6 inches of soil, and then to step into the hole and firm the soil at the base of the roots with your foot. Be careful, however, not to break any roots by stepping too close to the main stem of the plant. More soil should be added until the hole is filled to within 3 inches of the top, and then use a gentle trickle of water from the hose to fill the hole to the brim. When that water has settled, the rest of the hole can be filled in with the soil.

Once this is done, continue to add soil in a temporary mound around the stems of the plant. This mound will protect the stems from drying out before new growth is made and will preserve stem moisture during the period in which new roots are being formed. The soil mound should stay around the plants until the new buds grow to perhaps a quarter of an inch in length. If the soil mound is allowed to stay on until the soft new growth becomes an inch or so long, buds are apt to break off when the soil is removed. By examining the pale new shoots at regular intervals, you will be able to tell exactly when the mounding should be removed. You can remove most of the mound with a trowel, but wash the soil from among the canes with a gentle stream of water from your garden hose, so as not to injure the tender shoots.

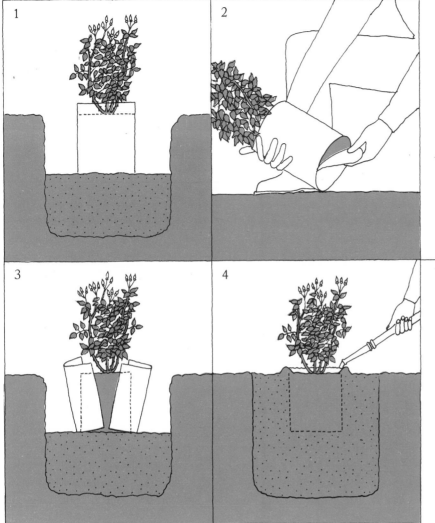

PLANTING A POTTED ROSEBUSH

1. *To plant a rosebush purchased in a tar-paper or metal pot, dig a hole twice the diameter of the pot and twice as deep as the height of the pot. Then fill the hole with soil mixed with fertilizer and peat moss until the pot, when set in the hole, has its own soil level even with the level of the ground.*

2. *After having watered the plant thoroughly—to make the soil adhere to the roots in one big lump—gently tip a tar-paper pot over far enough so that you can cut and peel away the bottom.*

3. *Place the pot in the hole, then cut the pot down both sides and pull it apart without disturbing the soil around the roots. (If the pot is metal, have it cut apart at the nursery and bound with twine; pull the halves apart, lift the plant out and set it in the hole.)*

4. *Fill the hole with soil, pressing it down to make it firm around the roots. Mold a trough about 1½ inches deep around the canes, then water until thoroughly soaked. Add 2 inches of coarse peat moss or other mulch to the soil surface around the plant.*

Potted rosebushes are planted with only minor variations from the procedures used for bare-root roses. But it is not necessary to build up a mound of soil around the bush after the planting has been completed. Follow the instructions that accompany the diagram above. The important thing is to remove the container and to set the plant into its hole without disturbing the cylinder of soil that surrounds the roots. Handled in this manner, a potted plant can be put into properly prepared soil at any time during the growing season without the risk of transplanting shock, even though it may be in full growth and perhaps even in bloom.

New plants, potted or bare-root, usually have wired onto one cane a tag that names the variety. For easy identification in the future, it is a good idea to save the tag and to add the planting date. The tag

TAGGING

can be fastened to a stake nearby, but never leave it on the plant, since the wire can squeeze the cane hard enough to choke off its growth and even to kill it in a single year.

PRUNING NEW BUSHES

Some gardeners feel that the planting operation is not complete until they have pruned their newly set bushes. Generally speaking, this practice is unwise. Before a rosebush is marketed, the upper plant is usually trimmed at the nursery to bring it into balance with the roots, which cannot support a larger top until they make new growth. Most newly set bushes require no further pruning at planting time, and should not be pruned for a full year. However, some bushes suffer minor injury in shipment or planting, and these may be pruned a little to compensate for the damage. If you have trimmed off two or three broken root ends while planting a particular bush, it is advisable to prune the longer canes of the upper plant slightly to bring it back into balance with the reduced root system. But the pruning of newly set plants—indeed of all the rose plants in your garden—should be done with great restraint.

CARING FOR ROSES

No matter how carefully you plant your roses, the plants cannot produce blooms unless they have an adequate supply of moisture and fertilizer to keep them actively growing, for only then do they send out flowers. This need will continue even after the plants are well established. With very few exceptions, the amount of food and water that must be given roses to stimulate a maximum amount of bloom is the same whether the bushes are old or new.

Water is usually the element in short supply, rather than fertilizer. Frequently there is still a considerable amount of plant food in the soil in midsummer, nutrients left over from spring feeding; however, unless moisture is present, the food cannot be assimilated by the plants. It is easy to see that the flush of bloom in both spring and fall coincides with the spring and the fall rains, when there is adequate moisture in the soil.

How much good ample water can do is indicated by an old story about a quack who traveled the New England countryside selling pink pills guaranteed, he said, to stimulate rosebushes into furious bloom. His prescription was one pill to a pail of water, administered once a week. It worked, too. Not that the pills did any good; the regular watering helped the roses so much that his customers never suspected they had been taken.

There is a simple way to tell if your roses need water. Stick your forefinger into the soil as far as you can. If it is dry down there, the roots below probably need moisture. Water thoroughly; the lowest roots will be properly moistened at about the time that the absorption of water slows down noticeably on the surface, usu-

ROSE FESTIVALS

Of the scores of rose shows held each year, a few have become full-fledged festivals, complete with parades, queens and attendant hoopla. The largest of these is the 10-day Rose Festival staged every June in Portland, Oregon, a major commercial growing center that calls itself the "Rose City." Others are the September Festival of Roses in Wasco, heart of the central California rose industry, and the Texas Rose Festival, an October fixture in Tyler, Texas. The best-known event of all, Pasadena's Tournament of Roses, provides fewer opportunities for the serious rose enthusiast, but is probably unmatched for its sheer display of blossoms, which cover the dozens of floats that wend their way through Pasadena streets on New Year's Day, prior to the Rose Bowl football game.

ally after about two hours. Such a soaking should serve for a week or 10 days under average conditions. After a week, make the finger test again, and repeat it daily until the next watering is indicated. Depending on the weather and the type of soil, you may water more often or less often, but do not vary the amount of water that you use in each application. A single deep watering does much more good than the same volume of water doled out in two or three superficial applications that only dampen the top of the soil.

Most gardeners simply water their plants by applying moisture to the surface of the soil; however, there are right and wrong ways of doing this simple task. It should be said at the beginning that it is advantageous to keep rose leaves dry because moist foliage encourages the spread of leaf-borne diseases. For that reason, complete the watering in early morning; this will give the sun a full day to dry out moist surfaces. To moisten the soil alone, rather than the leaves, use a hose that allows moisture to seep out along its length and soak into the ground—either porous canvas tubing through which water oozes, or a plastic "sprinkler hose" with many tiny holes for water to spray through. When the sprinkler hose is turned upright with the holes on top, the spray goes into the air, but in watering a rose bed, it is far better to turn it upside down (setting the water pressure low) so that all of the moisture will be directed into the soil. The job of watering can also be done with a long spray nozzle attached to an ordinary garden hose and aimed carefully at the soil around each plant. I have even seen thrifty gardeners water rose beds perfectly with an old sock fitted over the hose end. It may be a homely makeshift, but it does break the force of the water to prevent it from running away and to keep soil and mulch intact.

In the same breath that I mention water, I should also mention mulches because a mulch on top of the soil of the rose bed is the most effective way to conserve moisture. But a proper blanket of mulch, spread to a thickness of 2 to 4 inches depending on the kind you use, will do far more than conserve moisture. As insulation against the sun's rays, it will keep the soil as much as 10° to 20° cooler than that in an unmulched bed, providing the cool soil temperature in which roses grow best. It will deter encroaching weeds, which rarely germinate under a layer of mulch. It will give your garden a finished, picture-book look. And at season's end, when the mulch is partly decomposed, it can be worked into the soil as added enrichment or it can be left as a starting mulch for next year.

A mulch for roses may consist of nearly any type of organic matter. Peat moss is often used, but I suggest that you use only a very coarse grade of peat moss, not the finely ground type, which is best suited to mixing with dirt as a soil conditioner. Finely ground peat moss has a way of compacting after being in place for a short while and forming a practically waterproof cover over the ground. Other good mulching materials are shredded bark, leaves, pine needles, hay, ground corncobs, peanut shells, bagasse (sugar-cane pulp), cocoa-bean husks, buckwheat hulls, wood chips, or any other coarse organic material. Nurserymen who grow roses for florists mulch their rose beds with a mixture of straw and cow manure, which also acts as a fertilizer.

Whatever kind of mulch you use, it should be applied early in the season, and certainly before the sun gets really hot. Spread the material evenly over the bed. Most important, avoid putting mulch where it will touch the canes of the plant; this could cut down the air supply that the roots need or, during rainy periods, form a soggy mass that can rot the canes. One trouble with mulches is that they use up the soil's nitrogen as they decompose. If leaves turn pale green, the plant is short of nitrogen and a nitrogen-rich fertilizer should be applied.

When watering a mulched rose bed, there is no particular benefit in getting the mulch itself moist; it is the soil beneath that must be kept wet. Take a hoe or the toe of your shoe and dig a little trench in the mulch, then lay the hose in the trench. In this way the water will be directed down so that it will not be wasted saturating the organic material on the surface.

FERTILIZERS   In the good old days, fertilizer meant one thing to gardeners in general and rose gardeners in particular: well-rotted cow manure. They bought a load of that excellent but malodorous stuff, spread it thick over their rose beds and confidently waited for splendid results. The manure acted as a combination mulch, fertilizer and soil conditioner in a way that modern chemical concoctions seem unable to duplicate. Oddly, its nutrient content is comparatively meager —perhaps 10 to 20 per cent that of chemical fertilizers—and large amounts had to be used. But well-rotted manure contains microorganisms that make nutrients in the soil more accessible to the plants, nourishing them into vigorous growth and prolific bloom, and no other fertilizer wholly takes its place.

Nowadays farms are few in suburban areas, and it requires considerable effort and a little luck to find natural manure. Gardeners who still prefer organic fertilizer generally must settle for dried cow manure, bone meal, cottonseed meal, blood meal, fish fertilizer or thoroughly decomposed compost. But most gardeners today use chemical fertilizers, compounded to provide all the nutrients plants need. Some of these are sold especially for roses, but the ones for general garden use work well in my rose beds.

All fertilizers have three main ingredients, each of which helps a rosebush in a different way. Nitrogen stimulates green growth, producing more and bigger canes, stems and leaves. Phosphorus (listed on the label as phosphoric acid) stimulates root growth and increases flower production, while potassium (listed as potash) promotes vigorous growth so plants are better able to resist disease and cold. The chemical fertilizer used by most rose gardeners contains 5 per cent nitrogen, 10 per cent phosphorus and 5 per cent potassium, represented by the shorthand notation 5-10-5. Other fertilizers are compounded with different proportions of the three main ingredients in order to produce different effects. For example, a rose plant that is slow to begin new growth can be hurried along with nitrogen-rich fertilizer such as 10-10-5. A small additional amount of phosphorus, as in the formula 5-15-5, may help to strengthen weak stems having flowers that tend to hang their heads.

How often you fertilize depends partly on your plants and partly on climate. Newly set bushes do not require any spring feeding if their bed has been well prepared in advance. As a matter of fact, they are better off if not given additional food until after the appearance of the first flush of flowers. Mature plants, on the other hand, need fertilizer just before buds sprout in the spring. For them, scratch one-half cup of 5-10-5 per plant lightly into the soil, or, if you have already protected the soil with mulch, scatter the food evenly on top and water thoroughly. To keep roses growing luxuriantly through the season, treat both new and old bushes when the first wave of blooms has passed and again in midsummer, using one-fourth cup of fertilizer per plant each time.

This is all the fertilizer ordinarily given roses in the cold to moderate climates of Zones 3-7. Later feedings may stimulate soft new growth that is especially vulnerable to damage from frost. If a late feeding does seem necessary, use a nitrogen-less fertilizer, such as 0-10-5, which will nourish and toughen the plants without fostering the easily frozen new growth. In the warm climates of Zones 8-10, however, where winter hazards are not a problem, a late summer feeding is routine; this fourth application—one-third to one-half cup per plant—will guarantee lovely flowers all through the fall for gardeners in the Deep South and on the West Coast.

No discussion of rose fertilization would be complete without mention of foliar feeding. The term is applied to a fertilizing method in which a mixture of inorganic plant foods is dissolved in water and sprayed on the leaves of the plants. The fertilizer bypasses the root system because it goes directly into the leaves and is used by the plants immediately. It is particularly effective when applied to the undersides of the leaves because most of the stomata, or leaf openings, are located there. Foliar feeding is not a panacea; when

ATTAR OF ROSES

Attar of roses, a yellow-green oil distilled from rose petals and used for centuries in making perfumes, is so valuable (twice the price of gold) that Bulgaria, the major producer of the oil today, keeps hundreds of drums on deposit in foreign banks to maintain its international balance of trade. Bulgaria gets most of its attar from a central region some 60 miles long and 6 miles wide that is densely planted with roses, chiefly of the fragrant red damask type. The rose harvest begins in May and lasts for about three weeks; the cut flowers are loaded on carts and driven to 40 local distilleries. It takes about 4,000 pounds of roses to produce one pound of pure attar, which is packed in metal drums and sold to perfume manufacturers for up to $800 a pound.

adequate fertilizer and moisture are available in the soil, its advantage is mainly one of convenience. Foliar feeding is an easy and quick way to supplement midspring and midsummer feedings, particularly if blossom production seems to lag.

PEST CONTROL   One of the nice things about the foliar method of applying fertilizer is that the nutrient chemicals can be mixed with insecticides and fungicides so you can feed your plants and protect them from insects and diseases at the same time. For it is unfortunately true that roses are attacked by a host of different kinds of pests and diseases. Although some kinds are more disease resistant than others (*see the guide to pests and diseases on pages 54-57*), all rose plants need protection against their enemies, and pest control is an essential part of rose culture.

Over and over again gardeners tell me what a terrible chore it is to keep rose plants healthy, but this need not be true. A large part of pest control can be taken care of easily by maintaining healthy plants. Keep them well fed and well watered so that they are better able to resist attack, and rake off fallen leaves and petals that might harbor disease.

Regular attention with either sprays or dusts will keep healthy roses healthy. The key words are regular attention. You cannot wait until roses are covered with insects or fungi before inaugurating a program. Wise rose growers apply pesticides regularly once a week, starting early in the spring when growth burgeons and continuing throughout the season, cutting the application rate to once every two weeks in hot weather. Seldom is it necessary to go to the trouble of mixing your own insecticides and fungicides; buy a rose spray or dust that is formulated to control both insects and diseases and use it faithfully.

If you have only a few plants, you will find that dusting is easier than spraying because you do not have to clean the equipment after each use. Of the several kinds of dusters on the market, perhaps the most useful is a crank-operated device; you crank slowly to apply an even coating of dust to foliage nearby, faster to increase the range.

Spraying, however, is slightly more effective than dusting, and most gardeners who have more than a dozen or so bushes elect to spray. The equipment chosen should have a capacity large enough so that you can cover all of your plants without refilling. The types of sprayers suitable for home use include, in order of increasing capacity (1) atomizers operated by a plunger handle; (2) hose-end sprayers, consisting of a bottle and siphon tube that dilute and distribute pesticides under water pressure; (3) slide or trombone sprayers, operated by working a hand grip back and forth; (4) compressed air sprayers; and (5) electrically driven mist sprayers. Whatever size of sprayer your garden requires, the equipment must be washed out thoroughly after each use with plain water to prevent corrosion. The sprayer should never be used for applying weed killer; no matter how carefully you rinse it out afterward, the residual effect of the powerful chemicals will remain strong enough to burn garden plants. Since rose sprays also contain potent ingredients, it is important to follow the manufacturer's directions carefully when diluting and applying a solution.

Both dusts and sprays should be applied early in the morning. When dew is still on the plants, the dust clings to the leaves better than if the job were done later in the day. Spraying, however, should be delayed until the dew has dried; an application at about 10 a.m. gives the sun most of the day in which to dry the spray off the plants. Take extra care not to miss the undersides of leaves, where pests congregate.

While the regular application of any general-purpose rose spray will almost always control insects, mites and diseases, occasionally one or another of them becomes so established that specific measures are needed to control it. Certain pests, too, are more prevalent in some parts of the country than in others. For example, a gardener living in California need not worry about the Japanese beetles

PRUNING FOR MORE ROSES

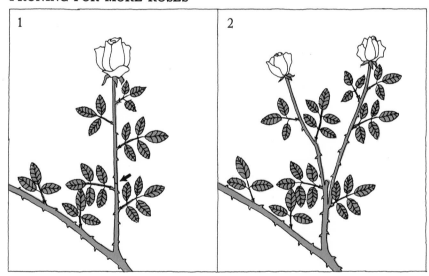

By pruning accurately you can increase the number of blooms a rosebush will produce. Make a diagonal cut on the stem about ¼ inch above the upper leaf of a pair of five-leaflet leaves (arrow).

Several weeks later, the properly placed cut has stimulated the growth of a new stem from the bud eye at the base of the upper leaf. Often a flowering stem will also grow from the base of the lower leaf.

A guide to pests and diseases

The first line of defense against garden pests and diseases that affect roses is good health: a well-fed, well-watered rose plant in a garden kept free of weeds, dead leaves and other debris is much less susceptible to attack and, when trouble comes, much better able to survive it. Even so, most rose gardeners regularly resort to a program of chemical applications, beginning in the early spring and continuing at one-week intervals throughout the growing season (although in hot weather it is best to lengthen the interval to two weeks, to guard against "burning" the plants).

The most convenient treatment is an all-purpose combination of chemicals formulated especially for roses and containing a pesticide, a fungicide and a miticide to control mites. This is commonly sold in powder applicator containers or pressurized spray cans for small jobs. Gardeners who have more than a half-dozen rosebushes generally buy all-purpose chemicals in larger

DISEASE	SIGNS OF INFECTION	MOST SUSCEPTIBLE ROSES
CANKER	Dark lesions or dead places occur, primarily on canes; they are caused by fungi that enter through pruning cuts (especially cuts made too far above bud eyes, leaving dead stubs) and through graft unions and places where thorns have been torn off. Cankers frequently circle plant stems in brown patches, thus cutting off the flow of nourishment and causing leaves and flowers above them to die.	hybrid teas hybrid perpetuals tea roses
CROWN GALL	A bacterial disease causing roundish, rough, tumorlike growths, crown gall is commonly found near soil level or on roots. Wounds from gardening tools and grafts make plants susceptible. Infected plants become stunted, lose vigor and die.	All classes
POWDERY MILDEW	A white or gray powdery coating appears on canes and leaf buds. Leaves curl and turn dry; buds shrivel before they can open. Most common of all rose diseases, this fungus is especially prevalent in humid weather, afflicting plants that grow too close together or receive too little sun.	hybrid teas floribundas climbers small-flowered ramblers
ROSE BLACKSPOT	Black spots form on leaves; tissue next to the spots turns yellow and leaves eventually fall off. The disease occurs mostly in humid weather and is spread by spores that form on spots and are carried from plant to plant by rain or sprinkling.	hybrid teas hybrid perpetuals polyanthas tea roses
RUST	Reddish orange pustules resembling warts appear on the undersides of leaves, which soon wither and drop. In autumn spores turn black, survive the winter and start a new cycle in the spring.	hybrid teas climbers hybrid perpetuals
SPOT ANTHRACNOSE	Leaves develop white spots with dark red rims; the spots eventually turn yellow, and the leaves become full of holes and fall off. Stems also develop raised brown spots with light colored centers. The fungus lives on through the winter in these spots, producing spores that are disseminated by rain in the spring.	climbers

amounts for use with garden-hose attachments, tank sprayers or dusting devices. Whatever you buy, check the formula, printed on the container, to make sure it includes the chemical most effective against the particular pest or disease from which you anticipate trouble. The labels specify chemicals by their common names, and it is these names rather than trade names that are listed on the chart (with the exception of the chemicals used for control of nematodes; these are more com-monly known by their trade names as listed).

Before using any gardening chemical read the label. Follow the instructions for dosages, and *observe all the precautions given*. No chemical should be used when wind can spread it, or near anyone who is eating, drinking or smoking. Many pesticides are poisonous to humans and household pets; others are unsafe to use around fish, birds and honeybees. Always store these products under lock and key, out of the reach of children.

CHEMICAL CONTROLS	OTHER METHODS OF CONTROL
Apply lime-sulfur spray immediately after pruning. Spray weekly through the growing period with folpet, captan, zineb, maneb or ferbam.	Since canker flourishes in dying tissue such as pruned stubs, always cut stems close to a bud or leaf. Prune off and burn cankered canes. Canker can be spread from plant to plant by infected shears: dip them in 70 per cent alcohol or formaldehyde between cuts.
Apply streptomycin, available in spray-powder form at garden stores, every two weeks during the growing season.	Remove and burn infected parts. When pruning, dip shears in formaldehyde or alcohol between cuts to avoid spreading the disease. Plant healthy bushes elsewhere in the garden.
Apply lime-sulfur spray before spring growth starts. Once a week during the growing season spray with cycloheximide, folpet, sulfur or dinocap. With the exception of folpet, do not use these chemicals when the temperature is above 85°F. or you may burn the plants' leaves.	Choose resistant varieties, such as shiny-leaved climbers. Avoid overcrowding and locations that are damp or shady. Water early in the day so that leaves have a chance to dry.
Apply lime-sulfur spray before spring growth begins; spray with folpet, captan, zineb, maneb or ferbam weekly throughout the growing season.	Water plants early in the day so that the leaves will be dry by nightfall. Remove diseased leaves and prune diseased wood before spring growth. Do not space plants too close together.
Spray in early spring with sulfur, ferbam, zineb, maneb or cycloheximide. Be sure to spray the undersides of leaves.	Choose resistant rose species such as polyanthas. Remove and burn infected parts. Space plants for good air circulation. Avoid wetting foliage any more than necessary.
Apply lime-sulfur spray in early spring while plants are dormant. Once a week during the growth period spray with captan, ferbam, folpet, maneb or zineb.	Prune infected stems in the spring.

PEST	DESCRIPTION	SIGNS OF
 APHIDS	These pear-shaped insects are usually wingless, of various colors and less than ¼ inch long. Roses are particularly susceptible to the rose aphid, which is green, and to the pink-and-green potato aphid.	Aphids often settle on new shoots, but are also found on the undersides of leaves, on stems or at the base of buds. They suck the plant's juices, causing leaves to
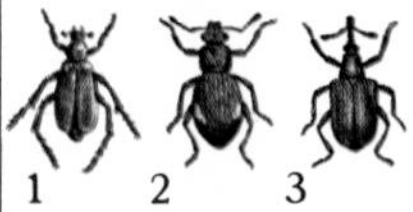 BEETLES	In addition to the familiar Japanese beetle, beetles harmful to roses include the rose chafer *(1 at left)*, ½ inch long and yellowish brown; the Fuller rose beetle *(2)*, grayish brown and less than ½ inch long; and the rose curculio *(3)*, ¼ inch long and colored red with a long black snout.	Beetles chew the foliage, stems and flowers of roses, making large round or irregularly shaped holes in the leaves and petals. The larvae feed on the plants'
 BRISTLY ROSE SLUGS	Bristly rose slugs—also called cane borers, leaf worms or rose caterpillars—are the larvae of saw-flies (which resemble horseflies but have four wings). The slugs are ½ inch long, greenish white, and are covered with stiff hairs. They are most active in early spring.	Larvae feed on the undersides of leaves, eating large holes through them. Left
 CATERPILLARS	Among caterpillars that feed on roses are the budworm, a greenish or whitish orange insect about ⅜ inch long, and the pale green rose-leaf tier, about ¾ inch long.	In late spring these types of caterpillars eat into flower buds; they will also pull
 EARWIGS	These night-feeding insects are dark brown, ⅝ to 1 inch long, and have rear pincers resembling ice tongs.	Earwigs attack rose petals and leaves,
 LEAFHOPPERS	Leafhoppers are elongated suckers, 1/16 to ¼ inch long, that fold their wings in a wedge shape. They may be colored light green, yellowish brown, yellow or white.	Leafhoppers work on the undersides of leaves, creating a white, stippled effect on the tops and causing the edges to curl as
 NEMATODES	Tiny, often microscopic animals, nematodes are colorless and resemble worms.	Nematodes feed mostly on roots, but also on stems, leaves and buds, causing stunting, lack of vigor and tumorlike
 ROSE MIDGES	Tiny (1/20 inch long), reddish or yellowish brown, these flies lay their eggs on new growth; the larvae feed on buds and leaves.	Buds and leaves turn black, become deformed and die. Full-grown larvae
 ROSE SCALES	Several varieties of this sucking insect attack roses; some look like gray or brown dots less than ⅛ inch in size; others resemble tiny, dirty white seashells about ¼ inch across.	Scales suck the sap of leaves and stems,
 SMALL CARPENTER BEES	These bees, also called pithborers, are about ⅓ inch long and are black in color with metallic highlights.	Carpenter bees bore into rose canes and lay their eggs in the pith; they hatch into
 SPIDER MITES	Eight-legged, spiderlike creatures, mites are about as big as a speck of paprika — 1/75 of an inch — and sometimes paprika colored, although they may also be green or yellow.	Mites thrive in hot humid weather in locations where air circulation is poor. They attack plants by sucking their juices, particularly from the leaves,
 THRIPS	Sucking insects, 1/20 inch long, thrips have slender orange-yellow or brownish yellow bodies and bristly fringed wings.	Thrips attack floral, stem and foliage tissue. Buds are either prevented from opening at all or open only partially;

INFESTATION	CHEMICAL CONTROLS	OTHER METHODS OF CONTROL
curl and flowers to be malformed, and transmit fungus and bacterial diseases. Aphids secrete a sticky substance called honeydew, which attracts ants to leaves.	Two or three times in the spring, at two-week intervals, apply oxydemeton-methyl, nicotine sulfate, rotenone, malathion or pyrethrum. Be sure to spray undersides of leaves.	
roots. Some beetles, including the Fuller rose beetle and the brown Asiatic garden beetle, feed at night.	Spray both plants and soil weekly with carbaryl, malathion or methoxychlor.	Pick off beetles by hand or knock them into a can of water covered with a film of oil or kerosene. Specially designed traps are sold in garden supply stores.
unchecked, they will eventually reduce the leaves to skeletons.	Spray two or three times in early spring with malathion, rotenone, carbaryl or methoxychlor. The spray should be applied to the undersides of the leaves.	Since bristly rose slugs in their cocoon stage tend to winter over in garden debris, a thorough fall clean-up is essential.
leaves around themselves and then eat their way through the leaves.	Apply carbaryl or methoxychlor weekly.	Pick off and destroy infested buds or clusters of leaves.
eating many small holes through them.	Earwigs hide during the day under wood piles, along fences and foundations; spray these hiding places with carbaryl.	Keep the garden free of dead leaves and other debris that serve as hiding places for the insects.
if they had been burned. When disturbed, the insects hop quickly away. Like aphids, they are carriers of virus diseases.	Spray weekly in spring and fall with dimethoate, carbaryl, malathion, methoxychlor, rotenone or pyrethrum. Be sure to spray the undersides of leaves.	
growths on roots. As a result of their wounds, plants become especially vulnerable to bacteria, rot and wilt.	Following manufacturer's instructions, treat the soil two to three weeks before planting or right after planting with DBCP or VC-13 Nemacide, whichever is recommended for your local soil.	Destroy sickly plants. Apply a thick organic mulch to the soil to discourage infestation.
drop to the ground, mature into flies in a week and start the cycle over again.	Spray plants and soil once a week throughout the blooming season with carbaryl, malathion or methoxychlor.	Remove and destroy the affected parts.
causing the plant to wilt and often die.	Before growth starts in the spring, apply a lime-sulfur or oil-emulsion spray. If scales appear, spray with malathion.	Cut off infested canes.
larvae that eat through the canes, causing the plant to wilt above the point of entry.		Tips of canes exposed by pruning should be sealed with cane dressing or tree paint. Wilted stems or canes should be cut off and burned.
causing foliage to appear stippled red, yellow, gray or brown. In addition, they often spin webs that line the undersides of leaves.	Starting in early spring, spray weekly for several weeks with aramite, dicofol, naled, rotenone or tetradifon. Be sure to spray the undersides of leaves.	If the infestation is not heavy, mites can be controlled by knocking them off the plants with a stream of water. Spring and fall garden clean-up wards off attack.
damaged petals turn brown at the edges. The insects are most attracted to yellow and other light colored roses.	Spray two or three times in early spring with carbaryl, malathion or dimethoate.	Remove infested blooms and buds.

that trouble rose growers on the East Coast, but he should keep a sharp lookout for thrips, which are known to invade the gardens of his area. To be ready for such special hazards, it is wise to know the rose's major enemies and when they strike; then it is relatively easy to identify one if it does appear and take the action that will eliminate it. The essential information on the most widespread and troublesome rose diseases and insect pests appears in the charts on the accompanying pages.

CUTTING FLOWERS

If you complete your spraying, feeding and watering on schedule, you should be able to spend much of your time in the rose garden doing nothing but admiring the flowers, or cutting some for the house. But there are even right and wrong ways to cut roses, for cutting determines the plant's growth pattern.

To cut a flower the right way, start out with proper equipment: sharp, clean scissors or shears and a pair of sturdy gloves as protection against thorns. Next, find the proper place to cut. If you examine a hybrid tea or any other rose plant that bears its flowers one to each stem, you will see what appears to be a small branch with five leaves on it. Actually, this whole growth is a single compound leaf. Above this five-leaflet leaf you will see three-leaflet leaves and single leaflets. But a five-leaflet leaf is the one most like-

DISBUDDING FOR FEWER, BIGGER BLOOMS

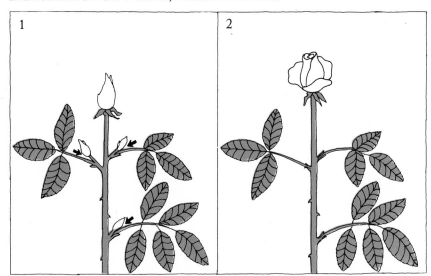

To produce bigger blooms for flower arrangements, allow the first rosebud to grow at the top of the stem, then pinch off the other buds with thumb and forefinger when they are about a quarter of an inch long (arrows).

Because it no longer must share the nourishment in the stem with the buds that appeared lower down, the remaining rosebud develops into a splendid flower that may be considerably larger than normal size.

ly to cover an eye or bud that is mature enough to develop into a strong flower-bearing stem. If you cut about a quarter-inch above the first five-leaflet leaf pointing outward, you direct the plant's energy to an incipient bud at the base of the leaf, one that will get a maximum amount of sunlight; it will grow rapidly into a stem that eventually produces a flower or flowers of its own. Sometimes the extra energy available in the stem stimulates a second, lower eye, and two flower-bearing stems grow where there had been one. If you cut too far above the five-leaflet leaf—say 2 inches rather than a quarter-inch—the extra length will die back, leaving an unsightly remnant through which boring insects may enter. Plants like floribundas and polyanthas, which bear clusters of flowers, should also be cut to stimulate continued flower production; as each bloom in a cluster fades, remove it from its stem, and when the last blossom in the cluster is gone, cut the stem back to a point a quarter of an inch above the first five-leaflet leaf.

Too much cutting, however, harms roses. A bloom cut with a long stem takes a large number of leaves; and in the spring, the reduced foliage may slow growth. After midseason, long-stemmed flowers can more safely be taken. But toward mid-September in the north it is best to stop cutting flowers off any kind of rosebush. By leaving the last roses on the plant, you permit seeds to develop

PRUNING TO REMOVE SUCKERS

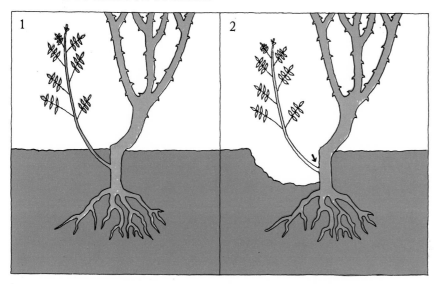

Sometimes the rootstock on which a hybrid rose is grown sprouts a cane, or sucker (above). Suckers can be recognized by their pale, small, often serrated leaves; if not cut off they can kill the hybrid top.

To remove a sucker, carefully dig to expose the rootstock. Unless the cane grows from beneath the bud union, it is not a sucker and should not be pruned. Cut off a sucker flush with the root trunk (arrow).

in the hip or seed pod beneath each flower. This signals the plant to settle into protective dormancy as colder weather approaches.

DISBUDDING While cutting helps maintain or increase the number of flowers a rosebush bears, another technique can control the size of blossoms on hybrid teas and similar varieties. "Disbudding," which requires removal of all but the top flower buds on each stem *(drawing, page 58),* concentrates the plant's energy into the remaining buds. The results are fewer but much larger blooms. Disbud while the flower buds growing from the base of a leaf are still very small—about a quarter of an inch long. They are then so soft that you can snap them off with a finger without leaving an unsightly stub.

REMOVING SUCKERS Whenever you cut blooms or disbud, keep a sharp eye for suckers *(drawing, page 59)*—fast-growing new shoots that sometimes emerge below the bud joint where the cultivated upper plant was budded onto the rootstock. These outgrowths can be identified not only by their point of origin but also by their small, finely serrated leaves. If you see one, cut it off as close to the rootstock as possible, even if you must pull away the soil to get at the base of it. A sucker that is allowed to grow unchecked will quickly dominate the upper plant, sapping its energy and eventually destroying it.

WINTER PROTECTION Suckers harm a rose during the growing season. But more serious damage can come from winter's cold. There is no sight that brings more dismay to the heart of a gardener in the springtime than to find his plants blackened and shriveled by winter weather. It is a heart-rending experience, and an expensive one as well, to lose fine rosebushes simply because of the season's bluster. A rose grower's idea of paradise is a place where wintry winds never blow, but few such places are to be found in this country, and many of the most delightful roses are descended from tender species that are easily damaged by wind and frost.

The extent of protection a rose needs depends not only on the kind of plant and the climate zone but may vary widely within a single neighborhood. One expert rose grower living in Hartford, Connecticut, reports that one of his climbing roses suffers little winter damage although it gets no protection except that offered by the shelter of his house, while in a park just a mile away, climbers of the same variety need heavy protection to survive. Any generality about winter protection requires many such qualifications.

Nevertheless, the climate zone in which you live *(map, page 153)* is the best guide to the steps necessary to safeguard your plants. In Zones 8-10—warm or moderate climates where temperatures seldom go below 10 degrees—it is unnecessary to protect any roses; all except possibly some tender tea roses should come through an average winter with little or no damage. In the moderate climates of Zones 6-7 where temperatures occasionally drop to zero or below, moderate protection is needed for most hybrid roses, bush types as well as climbers. In Zones 3-5, where subzero temperatures are common, only the hardiest varieties will survive a normal winter without some protection, and most hybrids will need heavy protection. (For comments on the hardiness of the popular types, see Chapter 4.)

A good first step is to coat each plant with an antidesiccant spray, which seals in moisture and combats the drying effects of the wind. The main danger to rosebushes in the moderate climates of Zones 6-7 is not cold itself but drying wind and frequent fluctuations in temperatures; repeated freezing, melting and re-freezing does far more damage to plant tissue than a single long-lasting freeze. In these zones, trussing the plants with evergreen branches or cornstalks wrapped in burlap may be enough to break the wind and hold out the cold.

This "Christmas tree" method is not always sufficient in moderate climates and is clearly inadequate in colder areas. The method of winter protection most commonly used everywhere north of Zone 8 consists of hilling soil around the canes. The soil should be brought

PROTECTING BUSH-TYPE ROSES IN WINTER

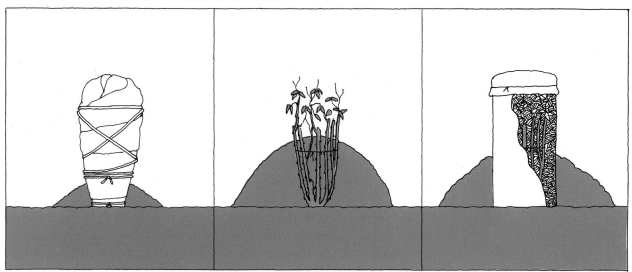

Even in moderate regions, it is wise to shield hybrid teas and other bush-type roses in winter against drying winds. Bind with evergreen branches or cornstalks and burlap, and mound 6 to 8 inches of soil around the base.

In the colder regions, as far north as Zone 3, the most common method of protection is to tie the canes together and mound a foot or more of soil in and around them. Bring in soil; don't rake it up from the base.

In Zones 3-5 where the winters are especially harsh, tie the canes together and enclose them in a tar-paper cylinder filled with peat moss or bark. Tie a burlap cover on top and mound soil around the base.

PROTECTING CLIMBING ROSES IN WINTER

1. *To protect a climbing rose in an area where winter temperatures dip low, but rarely below 10° (Zones 6-7), wrap it against cold winds in the fall. If the plant is trained to a post, first tie its canes close to the post with twine.*

2. *Next, wrap the canes in burlap, hay, straw or evergreen branches and tie these into a snug cover. Mound 8 to 12 inches of soil around the plant's base. If the climber has been trained along a fence or trellis, untie it and retie it to a post before wrapping it.*

In very cold areas (Zones 3-5), the best way to protect a climbing rose is to shield the entire plant with earth. Detach the climber from its support and tie its canes together. Then bend them to the ground, arching them near the plant's base to avoid breaking the canes; pin the canes down with crossed stakes. Mound soil over the entire plant, and drive a stake into the ground at each corner of the mound to mark the spot so the plant will not be trampled on. (Be sure that the stakes nearest the roots of the plant are not so close that they will cut into them.)

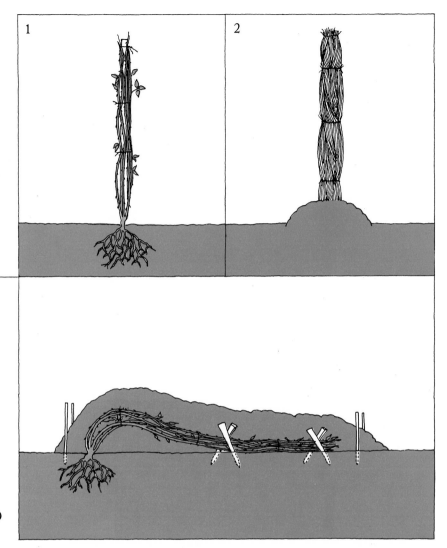

to the plants and not scraped from the surface of the beds, since this would only expose the rose roots to winter damage. The idea of mounding soil 8 to 12 inches high around the lower branches of a rosebush might be compared to buttoning up the collar of a winter coat. It keeps the canes of the plant from freezing just as a coat protects the body, but it cannot guarantee that the upper stems facing the winds without protection will not be frostbitten as easily as ears above a coat collar. Even worse, the soil mounds settle and erode over the winter, and canes thought to be covered become exposed to cold and drying winds.

A more satisfactory method of rosebush protection employs tall cylindrical collars, which are slipped over the tops of the plants and filled with loose material. Collars can easily be made at home from heavy tarpaper purchased at a hardware store and fastened to-

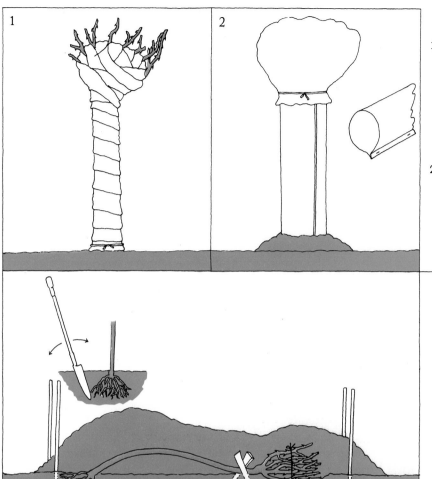

PROTECTING TREE ROSES IN WINTER

1. *To winter-proof a tree rose in the more moderate Zones 6 and 7, trim its top to a 10- to 15-inch crown. Wrap the trunk and its stake in stem-wrapping paper overlapped from the bottom up (so rain cannot seep in), until only the cane tips are exposed.*

2. *In the colder areas of Zones 3 to 7, wrap the tree as in the first drawing and then staple a cylinder of tar paper (inset) around it and tie burlap over the tree top. Mound soil to a height of 8 inches around the base.*

In the subzero cold of Zones 3 and 4, a still better way to protect a tree rose is to bury it. Loosen soil in a semicircle a foot from the tree base on the side away from the direction you will be laying the tree down. Dig the spade in to the depth of its blade and rock it back and forth (inset) to free the roots without exposing them. Remove the tree's stake and bend its trunk down close to the ground; dig a hole to rest the canes in. Peg the trunk to the ground with crossed stakes, cover the tree completely with soil and mark the location with stakes.

gether with heavy-duty staples. As a filling material, I prefer to use peat moss, ground bark or other mulch materials instead of soil; not only are they relatively light in weight and easy to use, but in the springtime they can be spread on the bed for mulch, while soil has to be carted to the beds in the fall and away from them in the spring. When the collars are filled, tie pieces of burlap over the top to keep the mulch in place.

It is a great temptation to use leaves as a winter covering for roses, either in the tarpaper collars or just piled atop the bushes. Lots of people do just that. But my advice is: don't. I speak from experience; one year when I was in a hurry I covered my roses with leaves and I lost several prized plants as a result. Some leaves carry disease organisms that can attack rose canes, and wet leaves induce rot, since they form a matted mass and keep moisture from draining.

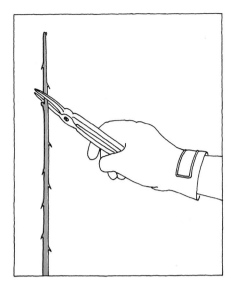

MAKING A PRUNING CUT

When pruning any kind of rose to remove winter-killed branches or to stimulate healthy growth, cut carefully lest the wound induce rot or attack by insects. Shears with two sharp opposing blades make a neater cut and squeeze slender stems less than shears of the blade-and-anvil type, which are more suited to heavier pruning; most rose growers also invest in a pair of heavy gloves to protect against thorns. Cut on a 45° angle to the stem axis, so that rain and dew will slide off the stem end rather than collect there and cause rot. Coat larger pruning cuts with rose cane dressing or tree paint to discourage stem borers.

A simpler and more convenient protective device than the collar is provided by foam-plastic domes that slip over the plants. It may be necessary to prune the bushes so they fit comfortably into the domes, but do not cut back any farther than is absolutely necessary. The domes must be firmly anchored by stones or soil on their bottom flanges or they are apt to be blown over by high winds. But they do not have to be filled with anything, they can easily and quickly be put into place in the fall and removed in the springtime, and they nest into one another like flowerpots for convenient storage. If you use them, I suggest you get the type with removable or hinged tops, which can be opened for ventilation during sunny days to prevent moisture from condensing inside.

While these techniques provide excellent safeguards for bush types of roses, the winter protection of climbing roses remains a challenge to a gardener's ingenuity. Their canes, too tall for collars or domes, are exposed to the full fury of winter unless a way is found to shelter them. Some gardeners take the canes down from their trellises or fences, peg them to the ground, and cover them with earth or mulch. Others bind the canes together and cover them with straw and burlap. These "mummies" are not particularly attractive, but they do help save climbers.

Even more troublesome are tree roses. They present a unique problem in winter protection in severe climates since they are 3 to 5 feet tall and their bud unions, from which the flowering portions of the plants grow, are located atop a main stem high above the ground. With the bud union, the weakest part of the rose plant, completely exposed to the elements, the tree rose becomes extremely vulnerable to winter damage. Some gardeners dig a trench on one

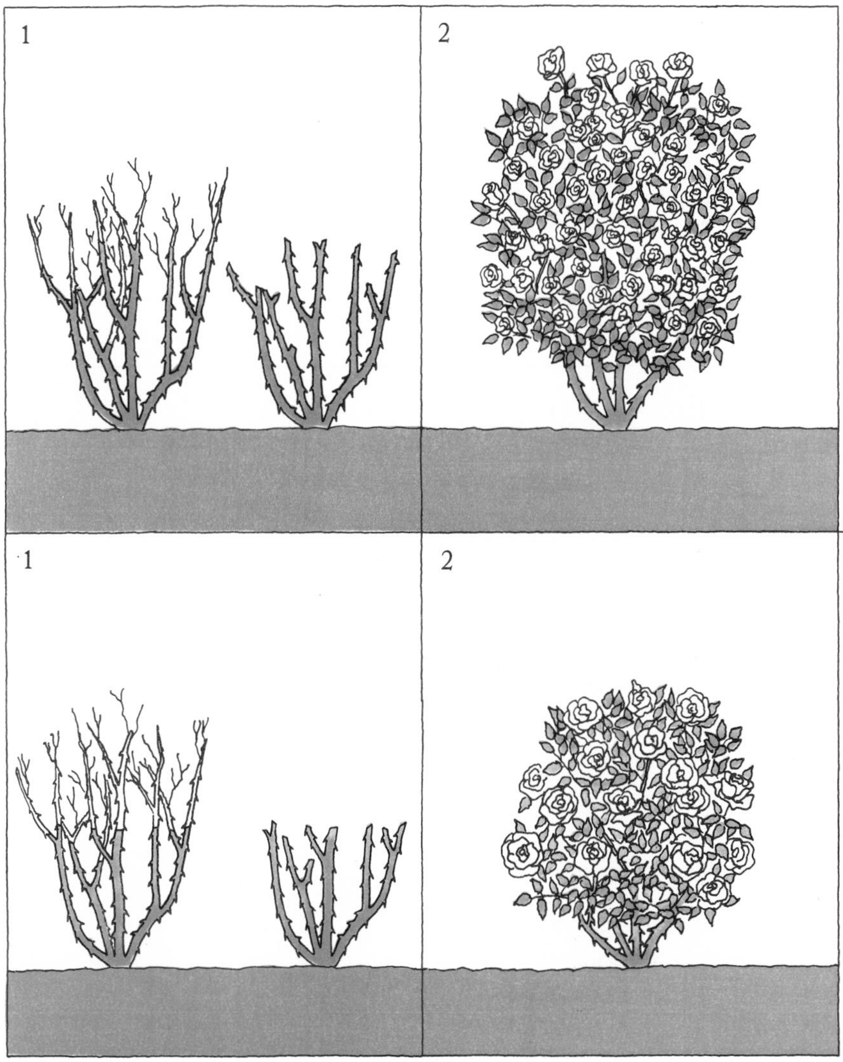

TWO WAYS TO PRUNE BUSH-TYPE ROSES

1. *The normal method for pruning a hybrid tea—or any modern bush-type rose, including floribundas and grandifloras—is to remove only the wood killed over the winter and the branches that, by crossing through the center of the bush, tend to rub against one another (uncolored sections).*

2. *The result of this "high pruning" is a bush that grows larger and fuller and produces more blooms than plants cropped by what is known as the "moderate" method, which is illustrated below.*

1. *In moderate pruning, winter-killed wood and cross-branching canes and stems are removed just as in high pruning, but in addition the healthy canes are then trimmed about halfway down to the ground, as shown in the right-hand part of the drawing.*

2. *The result of moderate pruning, followed by removal of incipient blossoms lower down on the stems through disbudding (page 58), is a bush with relatively few blooms, but of the large size desired for exhibition purposes as well as impressive cut flowers.*

side of each tree rose, loosen and partially dig up the roots from the opposite side, and bend the whole plant down to the ground. Then they cover the entire plant, roots and top, with a mound of soil and leave it there until springtime. This is a drastic operation, and it is also a laborious one, yet it is the simplest and easiest way that tree roses can be brought through the winter in very cold climates. But there are really no limits to the lengths a true lover of tree roses will go. A man in New Hampshire recently described how his tree roses, now 15 years old, have been protected each winter. He digs his plants completely out of the ground in the fall, lays them to rest in a deep trench and covers them over with soil; in the spring he dis-inters them and plants them once more, just as though they were newly purchased plants.

It is hard to tell exactly when to remove the winter protection. Coverings should be taken off before the plants make soft new growth, which can break in the removal process; this danger is greatest when the hilling method of protection has been used, and extreme caution is necessary in separating the loose soil from the plant. But spring arrives in capricious fits and starts, especially in regions with moderate climate. The soil mound should be removed as soon as you can see the plant's buds starting to swell. This usually happens long before the last frost is expected, so try to do the job when a period of mild weather is predicted. That way, the new growth will have a chance to become acclimated to its exposure and will be better able to resist injury from late frosts. Some growers prefer to remove the mound a little at a time over a period of several weeks, but this slower technique takes so much of a gardener's time that it does not seem warranted to me.

PRUNING

When the winter protection has been removed for the year, the condition of the plants will shock many a northern gardener who set out his first bushes the previous spring. The tops of tender varieties are often dark, mottled and shrunken, evidence of winter-killed tissue that must be removed to restore the plant to vigorous growth. By the time all the dead wood has been cut away, a plant may be even smaller and less promising than it was on planting day.

HOW TO PRUNE RAMBLER ROSES

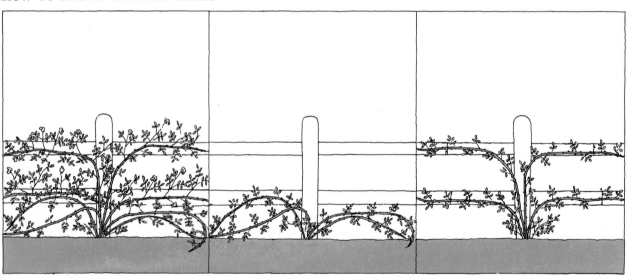

To prune a rambler, be careful to distinguish between the current season's flower-bearing canes—the one-year-old growth, tied to fence rails above—and the new growth, the canes trailing along the ground.

When the plant has finished blooming, in late summer, prune only canes that have borne flowers. Trim close to the ground, cutting the sections short to facilitate their removal from the thorny mass.

Tie the new growth in place; the four canes shown on the fence will produce next season's blooms. Still newer shoots are emerging at the plant's base; when they become large enough they should also be tied up.

The removal of winter-killed branches generally finishes the entire pruning job for gardeners in the north. Not so for those who live in warm climates. They must trim away some of their bushes to control their growth and insure good crops of well-formed flowers. But how much to cut away and when to cut it is argued vociferously among expert growers. Some urge drastic pruning, others are equally convinced that the less the better. Some, particularly in colder areas, prune in the fall, on the theory that many branches will be killed by winter cold anyway, but I think they are wrong.

In warm climates, fall pruning may work well, but the only fall pruning I do is designed to adjust the size of the plant to its winter covering. I get the best results by pruning in the spring. And I recommend that roses of every variety, in all climate zones, be pruned just as the plants' dormancy period ends and the new buds begin to swell. The actual time when this happens will vary, of course, ranging from January in very warm climates to as late as April in the cold northern zones. But the gardener who prunes too early runs the risk of additional frost injury after the job is done; pruning too late, after leaves have developed, results in a loss of sap from cut surfaces that can weaken the plants. So watch for the buds; when you see them beginning to swell, go ahead and remove growth that is hazardous to the plants' health: dead wood, weak

HOW TO KEEP A CLIMBER BLOOMING

To stimulate so-called continuous-blooming or everblooming climbers to produce flowers repeatedly all season long, the top of each stem (uncolored portion) should be pruned off after the blossoms fade.

Make the cut a quarter of an inch above the second five-leaflet leaf from the bottom. Slant the cut upward on the side toward the leaf to avoid damaging the bud eye, the source of a new flower-bearing stem.

Within six or seven weeks a new stem should grow out of the bud eye above the higher leaf, and often one will also grow out of the lower one. Repeated pruning as flowers fade will ensure repeated blooming.

branches, and infected stems and canes, which can be identified by the symptoms listed in the disease chart on pages 54-57.

How much more of a rosebush to remove depends on the type involved and on the gardener's own goals. Each type of rose needs to be thinned in a somewhat different manner, as indicated in the diagrams on these pages. And some types—notably the hybrid teas, grandifloras and similar bush-type roses, which predominate in modern gardens—can be pruned in either of two ways: "high" (very little) or "moderate" (up to one half the length of all canes), the choice being determined partly by climatic conditions and partly by the growth habit desired. The methods used and the results obtained are similar for all bush-type plants, but since hybrid teas are far and away the most popular type, the pruning techniques used on them serve as good examples.

Hybrid teas that are pruned back moderately respond by sending out a limited number of more vigorous shoots, each of which terminates, if disbudded by the technique shown on page 58, in a single large flower. I do not recommend pruning more drastically. Even if very big exhibition roses are your goal *(Chapter 3),* prune off no more than half the bush and you will have a larger, healthier plant that bears more perfectly shaped large flowers. Rigorously pruned rosebushes have fewer flowers, both at the first flush of

PRUNING A TREE ROSE

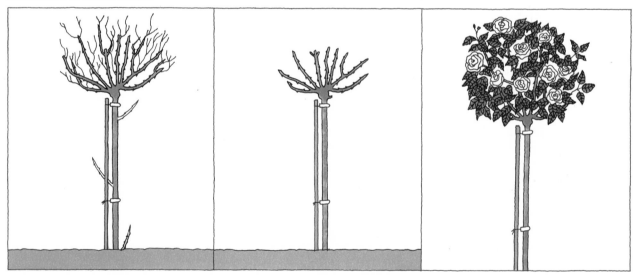

A tree rose, because it is a grafted composite, may produce numerous nonblooming suckers (uncolored branches) below the uppermost bud union. These should be cut back as close to the trunk as possible.

The top of the tree rose shown in the example above is a hybrid tea. Prune it just as you would any hybrid tea, cutting out all the dead and diseased wood and trimming the healthy canes back to a symmetrical shape.

If the pruning has been properly done the leafed-out top of the tree rose will become a luxuriant, globe-shaped crown of foliage and blossoms that provides a handsome vertical accent in the garden.

bloom and throughout the season, than do plants pruned more moderately. What is more, such drastic pruning produces coarse flowers and reduces the food supply that is stored in stems, and continuous cutting back year after year lessens the vigor of the bushes.

In high pruning, the entire bush is not cut; rather, trimming is limited to the growth made during the previous season, and these canes are cut back one half to two thirds their length. This method produces great quantities of lovely roses throughout the summer and fall. It also has the advantage of keeping most plants from getting too large so that more varieties can be grown in a given area. However, rose varieties differ dramatically in their growth habits, even within the hybrid tea class, and if really vigorous varieties are cut back as much as one half, they will send forth fast-growing succulent shoots that bear relatively few flowers. For them even moderate pruning may be too much. It is far better to treat plants of all types according to the habit of growth each individual variety displays. When you prune a naturally tall-growing variety, exercise special restraint; do not, for example, endeavor to cut it back to match the height of other varieties with a low growth habit. The average heights of many varieties are given in Chapter 4 so that you may plant and prune your roses with this as a guide.

When you prune, keep in mind that it is desirable to allow as

PRUNING A SHRUB ROSE

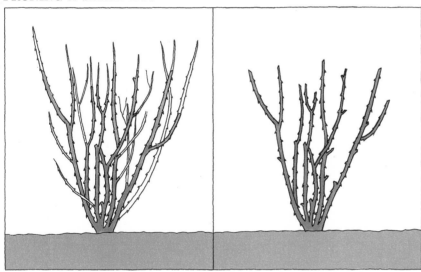

Since shrub roses are grown for their height—often as hedges—pruning is usually minimal; cut away the dead wood, and any overlapping branches and winter-killed cane tips (uncolored sections above).

The result, before any new growth begins, should look like this. After the shrubs have bloomed, do not cut the faded flowers. In the fall and winter they will provide a crop of bright, attractively colored rose hips.

much sunlight and air as possible to reach into the center of the plant, preventing the dank darkness that favors disease. Canes that are growing inward into the center of the bush should be removed carefully, especially if they are rubbing on other canes. And pruning cuts should be made just above an outward-pointing bud so the new growth will be started in the right direction.

If you live in a warm climate where there is little if any winter-killed wood to remove, even the moderate pruning method may trim off too much. Here it is best to limit pruning of hybrid teas to the removal of weak stems, which would use the plant's energy unproductively, and the cutting back of canes to the point where they are the thickness of a pencil. Such pruning will give the greatest amount of flowers over the longest blossoming season. However, additional pruning may be needed to counteract the hybrid teas' tendency to grow tall and leggy—that is, with few stems and scanty foliage close to the ground. This unfortunate habit of growth can be corrected to a certain extent by cutting the plants back rather severely from time to time to force new shoots to start from their bases. A better idea is to remove close to the ground level each springtime any canes that are four years or more in age. This will ensure the continued production of base stems.

As the accompanying diagrams show, other types of plants

PRUNING ONCE-BLOOMING, LARGE-FLOWERED CLIMBERS

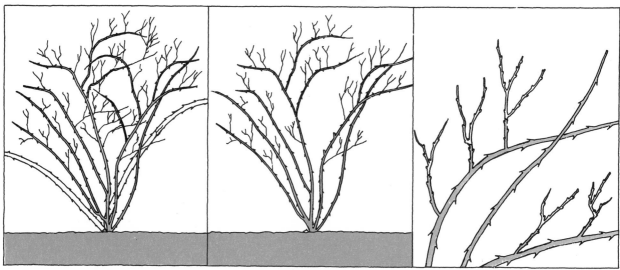

To stimulate blooming in roses of this type (page 120), first cut back canes that are five years old or more, like the ones shown uncolored above. Trim close to the ground in spring before the blooming season starts.

Remove dead or diseased canes and branches that cross in the center so that the bush appears much as it does above. (To show the pruning clearly, the climber is pictured here without any support behind it.)

As indicated in this enlarged detail of the upper right-hand section of drawing 2, prune the tops of the smaller stems (uncolored sections), leaving three or four bud eyes on each stem to produce flowers.

are pruned in a manner different from that recommended for hybrid teas. Shrub roses are so hardy they have little winter-killed wood to remove, and so are miniature roses. On the other hand, cluster-blooming plants such as the floribunda types require an almost continuous pruning operation, first to remove blooms as they fade and then to remove old stems and canes as they pass their best flower-bearing age. Old canes must also be removed from some climbing types. Large-flowered climbers produce most of their blossoms from canes that are less than four years old, and ramblers from canes that are only one year old; the process of removing the over-age growth keeps the plants young and free-flowering. Such canes should be cut off as close to the ground as possible.

The actual work of pruning is quite simple. Arm yourself with protective gloves and sharp, clean pruning instruments. Several types of shears are on the market. Some have two sharpened blades that work like an ordinary scissors; these are best even for heavy pruning. Others, the anvil shears, have one sharp blade that cuts against a blunt metal bar; these cut through thick branches easily, but they crush the delicate cells of rose canes. If you grow climbers and ramblers, you may also need long-handled lopping shears to reach growth high atop a trellis or arbor. For especially old, tough canes, a small saw is required. All of these implements should be kept sharp to avoid squeezing or tearing that will damage the branches, and if you are pruning away infected wood, dip them into a 70 per cent alcohol solution after each use.

Each pruning cut should be made cleanly, firmly and at the correct angle, as shown in the diagram on page 64. Many gardeners seal off pruning cuts using substances sold for this purpose by garden supply centers—cane sealer, rose paste and tree-wound paint. Wound paints made especially for roses are also available in aerosol spray cans. If you have the time, it is worthwhile sealing cuts in stems or canes that are larger in diameter than a lead pencil. When smaller stems are cut, this procedure requires more work than the results justify. Before you apply a sealant or move on to the next bit of pruning, check the pruning cut to make sure you have removed all the dead or diseased wood. The pith inside healthy growth is creamy white in color. If you see brownish pith, cut back to lower buds until the pith shows white.

One caution: don't get carried away by the pruning process; the gardener who prunes best is the gardener who avoids pointless extremes. But neither should you be intimidated by it. Nothing more than common sense is involved in all the techniques of rose culture—feeding, watering and spraying as well as pruning. If you follow the steps, one at a time, your home and your garden will be bright with blossoms all season long.

ROSE REMEDIES

Roses have figured prominently in many ancient home remedies, and even in black magic. For a sore mouth, a medieval doctor prescribed a hot potation made of ground rose petals and peppercorns. The Crusaders used a salve made of red roses to treat their battle wounds. Four pounds of roses went into a batch of ointment that, an 18th Century Englishman alleged, would relieve aches and strains in man or beast. Quite different powers were claimed for powdered rose petals and mustard seed mixed with the fat of a green woodpecker, according to a 12th Century English account. If a man applied this concoction to a neighbor's fruit trees, the recipe stated, it would stop them from bearing fruit forever.

The romance of the rose

Of all flowers, none has been so entwined in men's hearts and history as the rose. Roses lent their legendary romance to the Garden of Eden, to the Hanging Gardens of Babylon and to the gardens of ancient Persia, where nightingales sang and the clovelike scent of damask roses filled the air. The rose was the flower of Aphrodite, Greek goddess of love and beauty, and in Roman times it became the flower of Venus as well. Ever since, in the odes of poets and lays of balladeers, the rose has stood for womanly perfection and the mysteries of love.

Among the first women of history to capitalize on this symbolism was Cleopatra, who, the story has it, welcomed Marc Antony in a room filled with rose petals up to their knees. It was not long before Antony's countrymen outdid the Queen, importing shiploads of roses from Egypt for their pleasures. When Roman nobles dined, their guests were draped with rose garlands, washed with perfumed rose water, and plied with rose puddings and rose wine. In Rome the rose eventually became a symbol of debauchery and, somehow, of secrecy too: when Romans wanted to signify that a conversation was to be confidential, they hung a rose above the participants. Thus was born the term *sub rosa*—under the rose.

With the rise of Christianity the rose took on quite different associations. The white rose became a symbol of the Virgin Mary; the briar rose was said to have sprung from Christ's blood as He wore the crown of thorns. The glorious focal point of Gothic cathedrals, the stained-glass rose window, was patterned after the flower's radiating petals. The secular world soon adopted the rose as a favored device—in the banners of the Wars of the Roses, in the royal emblem of the Tudor monarchs and the highest awards of Victorian empire *(page 79)*, in stamps and coins the world over.

Today the rose has lost most of its more elaborate connotations, but its role as a romantic symbol continues undiminished. He who gives a single rose, or a dozen, speaks a universal message. And it may be no coincidence that June, the month of roses, has always been the month of brides.

In a rose-bordered 18th Century Persian miniature, a nightingale is perched on the stem of an outsized damask rose.

The roses of an ancient world

The rose was an ancient flower long before the first men appeared on earth. Fossil specimens, like the one at right, indicate that the flowers bloomed in what is now the American West millions of years before the oldest known picture of a rose was painted on a Cretan wall *(right)* during the Bronze Age 36 centuries ago.

In ancient Greek literature, the rose acquired a powerful mystique. Homer wrote in the *Iliad* that roses decorated the shield of Achilles and the helmet of Hector when they fought their mortal duel during the Trojan War. King Midas of Phrygia, legendary possessor of the golden touch, is said to have grown magnificent 60-petaled specimens in his gardens. It is believed that many islands of the Mediterranean were once covered with wild roses, including several varieties of *Rosa gallica*, the oldest identifiable rose and the basic ancestor of all modern roses. The name of one island, Rhodes, in fact comes from *rhodon*, the Greek word for "rose." Early in their history, the seafaring Rhodians adopted the rose as their symbol, and stamped it on many of their coins *(opposite page, top)*, which were widely circulated and used as currency throughout the length and breadth of the Mediterranean.

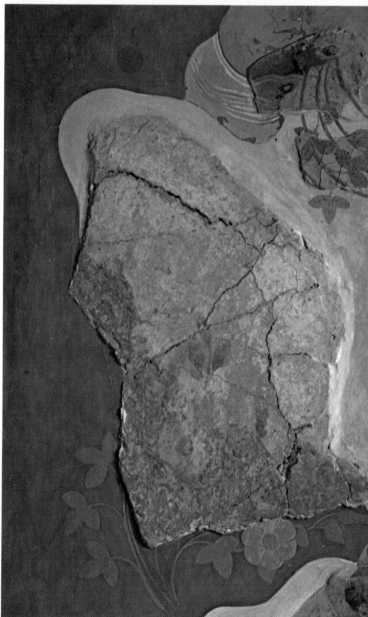

Several roses, drawn erroneously with six petals instead of the five possessed by most wild varieties, appear on a fragment of a 16th Century B.C. fresco from Knossos, Crete. The earliest known painting of a rose, it is believed to depict a Rosa gallica.

This fossil imprint of a rose leaf (left), about 40 million years old, was unearthed in Colorado and is the oldest known rose remnant. Botanists believe that roses evolved 60 million years ago, probably in Asia, and spread over most of the world.

A coin from ancient Rhodes, minted around 325 B.C., displays a rose, then the island's traditional floral symbol. Roses appeared on 102 different Rhodian coins over a period of several centuries until the island was conquered by Rome in the First Century B.C.

Floral symbol of Christianity

The rose was shunned by early Christians, who linked it with the excesses of pagan Rome. Prudentius, a Christian poet, wrote that the Third Century Spanish martyr St. Eulalia scorned the "sweet smell of roses" as she did jewels and other worldly pleasures. But by the Middle Ages, the rose had undergone a transformation in the eyes of the Church, becoming not only the symbol of purity of the Virgin Mary, but the model for a papal award and the inspiration for the magnificent stained-glass windows of the imposing Gothic cathedrals of Europe.

A golden rosebush 27 inches high, a symbol of papal benediction, was presented to the Italian city of Siena in 1463 by Pope Pius II. The blue jeweled dewdrop is thought to represent the Pope's gratitude to his home city.

Tinted light glows through the 13th Century rose window of the Cathedral of Notre Dame in Paris. Stained-glass "petals" in the shape of a rose radiate from a central figure of Christ.

An emblem of many nations

At one time or another, many nations have used the rose to lend beauty and dignity to their currency and their highest awards. Roses have appeared frequently on English coins since 1344, when Edward III first incorporated the flower's outline into the design of a gold coin that became known as the "noble" *(far right, top);* the rose-embossed Rosa Americana, shown behind the noble, was specially minted for use in the American colonies in 1722.

While the rose has been used simply for decoration, as in the gaudy three-dollar bill below, it often has had symbolic meaning as well. On the stamps shown here, the rose evokes the heroism of Russian polar explorers, the faith of a Peruvian saint, and sorrow for a dead Indian leader. Roses on medals, like those at the bottom of the opposite page, usually symbolize the highest achievement. In the Brazilian medal shown at right above, however, the garland of roses also represents the compliment of an emperor to the fair beauty of his bride.

Brazil's Order of the Rose, established by Emperor Pedro I in 1829, bears small enameled roses said to match the fair complexion of his wife, Princess Amelia.

A trio of rose-laden cupids adorns the face of a three-dollar note issued by a Kansas territorial bank in 1856.

The ubiquitous rose has appeared on the stamps and coins of far-flung nations. The stamps below, from left, commemorate the rescue of a 1938 Russian polar expedition, the 350th anniversary of the birth of St. Rose of Lima, and the first anniversary of the death of Jawaharlal Nehru. The English coins at right are decorated with stylized roses: an open-rose pattern on a gold noble and a stylized Tudor rose on the face of a Rosa Americana coin.

Enameled gold roses grace two of Great Britain's most prestigious decorations: the 600-year-old Order of the Garter (left) and the Order of the Indian Empire.

A portrait of Queen Elizabeth I, last of the Tudor line, shows her with roses on the lace collar of a gown covered with jeweled rosettes.

A suit of rose-embellished armor was worn at state ceremonies by George de Clifford, the Third Earl of Cumberland and one of Queen Elizabeth's court favorites.

England's national flower

No nation is more closely associated with the rose than England. Her great civil war, the 15th Century War of the Roses, got its name from the insignia of the rival families: the red rose of Lancaster, the white rose of York. After the war, which raged for 30 years, Lancaster's Henry VII married a York princess and united the families in a new Tudor dynasty. It was under the Tudors that the rose officially became England's national flower. The royal emblem was the Tudor rose, whose red and white petals symbolize the two reconciled houses.

The royal coat of arms of Great Britain symbolizes England by a lion and a rose, Scotland by a unicorn and thistle.

DIEU · ET · MON · DROIT

A huge Tudor rose adorns a version of King Arthur's legendary Round Table, 18 feet across, that was placed on the wall of Winchester Castle's great hall by King Henry VII to celebrate the birth of his son Arthur in 1486. Spokelike segments are marked off for the pictured king and his knights, whose names appear around the rim.

The death of Lancaster's Earl of Warwick, seen at right being struck by the lance of King Edward IV of York, is illustrated on a page from a 15th Century history of the Wars of the Roses. In the background a banner bears York's white rose on a red field.

The empress of roses

Perhaps history's most ardent devotee of the rose was Empress Josephine, wife of Napoleon I. In the magnificent gardens of the Château Malmaison, the setting for the family portrait below, she attempted to grow every known variety of rose. At the time of her death in 1814, she had collected some 250 different types, many of which live on in a series of splendid engravings *(opposite)* that she commissioned so that posterity would be able to see and admire her beloved roses.

Empress Josephine, the celebrated possessor of one of history's greatest rose collections, was depicted in this 19th Century engraving wearing, appropriately, a coronet of pale roses.

In "La Rose de la Malmaison," French artist Jean-Louis Vigier portrayed Emperor Napoleon offering a rose to his Empress as she sat in her garden with her relatives and ladies in waiting.

A magnificent specimen of a Rosa gallica aurelianensis from the gardens at Malmaison (opposite) was painted by Pierre-Joseph Redouté, official flower painter to Empress Josephine.

Rosa Gallica Aurelianensis   *La Duchesse d'Orléans.*

P. J. Redouté pinx.   Imprimerie de Rémond   Langlois sculp.

Creating better blooms 3

While Napoleon was off conquering Egypt in 1799, his wife Josephine bought an old château named Malmaison eight miles down the Seine from Paris. Napoleon grumbled loudly about the extravagance (apparently Josephine was outrageously overcharged for the property), but to modern rose growers the country estate was worth every sou it cost. For Malmaison made the rose the preeminent flower it is today. Here varieties from all over the world were collected and cultivated, while new, scientific techniques for breeding were developed. And Josephine's passion for roses *(pages 82-83)* set an example for the *haut monde,* so that roses became the fashionable flower to grow, and rose gardens were soon an essential accessory of the estates of the rich.

While Malmaison was a show place of many kinds of exotic plants and animals from all over the world (the menagerie included kangaroos, a chamois, an ostrich, and a trained orangutan that wore a coat and skirt, curtsied, and ate at a table), its roses were Josephine's first interest. More than 200 varieties grew in its gardens. Watching over them was a corps of horticulturists and botanists, including a consultant from London, nurseryman John Kennedy, who made regular visits to Malmaison despite the wars between England and France—he had a special pass to get safely through the lines of the opposing forces.

The remarkable results these experts achieved can still be seen, at least in part, for although Josephine's rose gardens fell into ruins after her death, they have now been largely restored, and Malmaison has become a public museum. Today an empress' resources are no longer needed to grow unusually beautiful roses or even to create wholly new varieties of plants. The techniques developed at Malmaison have been improved, simplified and added to so that home gardeners can grow spectacular "show" roses, propagate plants of their own and even breed totally new varieties.

Growing large and perfectly formed blossoms to compete in the organized rose shows that are held every summer in most parts

Blossoms of the grandiflora Duet dominate a field in Tyler, Texas, where nearly half of the rosebushes sold in the U.S. are grown. A rare blend of soil and climate makes the Tyler area an ideal one for rose propagation.

of the country requires advance preparation, careful cultivation—and a first-rate bush of a variety suited to show purposes. Hybrid teas are most frequently used, and among them the symmetrical, high-centered, large-petaled varieties such as Mister Lincoln and Chrysler Imperial *(Chapter 4)* are particularly favored by exhibitors. The techniques involved in producing flowers for competition are little different from those ordinarily employed for rose cultivation, and skill develops rapidly. I can recall a few gardeners who won prizes with the very first blooms they showed, and several other beginners who would have won had they followed more closely the finicky regulations for showing roses. For information on the two national shows held each year, write the American Rose Society, 4048 Roselea Place, Columbus, Ohio 43214. Local shows are often announced in the society's magazine, *The American Rose.* You need a show schedule because you have to plan your strategy, and the planning begins with the selection of a show to enter. Choose one that will be held conveniently nearby at a date that gives you time in which to complete preparations.

The work of producing a rose for show begins in the early spring. The goal is to grow a flower that comes close to the ideal features of its variety, represented by a perfect score of 100 points. The bloom must be typical in form and true in color; each of these qualities can earn a perfect flower 25 points. A stiff, straight stem and full, well-shaped leaves together are valued at 20 points; substance—the firmness and crispness of the petals—is worth another 20 points. The least important of the five judging standards is size of bloom, which counts for only 10 points.

The first step toward this goal is taken during the springtime pruning process. For a long time, it now turns out, people went about this the wrong way. They thought that cutting the plant back until almost nothing was left growing aboveground would stimulate it to grow a few exceptionally large blossoms. But not long ago skeptical nurserymen conducted comparison tests. They discovered that all they achieved with hard pruning was damage to the plant. The best roses appeared if the bush was pruned just slightly more than average, using the moderate method discussed in Chapter 2. As the flower-bearing stems grow, keep the number of buds on them to a minimum to encourage the development of large flowers, disbudding as shown in the diagram on page 58. It is necessary to follow very rigidly the culture routine outlined in Chapter 2, fertilizing, watering and spraying on a regular schedule. Ample water is essential, as is careful spraying—any damage from disease or insects will ruin the appearance of a rose. But don't make the mistake of applying too much of anything. Some people try to stimulate blooms to grow very large by dosing them with extra amounts of fertilizer; the results are coarse, poorly formed blooms. But if the recommended regimen is adhered to religiously for about 60 days after pruning, the buds of a good hybrid tea will begin to unfold into big, well-formed blossoms.

About a week before the exhibition date, keep your eye on two or three buds that seem likely to open just in time for the show. Single hybrid tea blooms are supposed to be displayed one-half to three-quarters open, and you can plan your flower cutting with this factor in mind. Cut all the good blossoms that are not more than one-third open in the early morning or late afternoon of the day before the show (you will select the best one of the lot at the show). The stems should be 18 inches long. Immediately put them in water and place in your refrigerator. The chill will prevent the flowers from opening too quickly. On the day of the show, take them out of the refrigerator, wrap them loosely in wax paper and transport them to the show in a long florist's box. (If a desirable bud begins to open too soon on the bush—say three or four days before the show—you can slow the opening by cutting the flower then, wrapping the bud in a soft cloth, and storing it in water in your refrigerator until the day of the show.)

At the show, correctly filled-out entry forms, proper labeling and display style are just as essential to a winner as a thoroughly manicured blossom at the peak of perfection. The judges look for any disqualifying fault that will help them narrow the field. If your blossom is still in the running at the end, the judges will ask themselves the ultimate question: "Is this a better and more typical Mister Lincoln bloom than that one is a Chrysler Imperial?" If you lose, try to find out why. The judges, if they have time, will often explain, and many are glad to give helpful advice for the next time.

PROPAGATING PLANTS

A different kind of excitement—and different challenges—await the gardener who turns to experimental rose growing. Any gardener who has space for more roses can easily grow additional plants from parts of bushes he already has on hand. Such a segment will, if properly treated, grow roots of its own, reproducing its parent by what is known as vegetative propagation.

The offspring will be an exact duplicate of the parent—in contrast to plants propagated sexually, from seed; seed-grown roses resemble their parents no more than human offspring do. One caution: Most garden varieties are protected by plant patents, which give the breeders the right to control the duplication of their plants for 17 years; unauthorized propagation of a plant still covered by a patent is a violation of the law.

The easiest way to reproduce rosebushes vegetatively is by cutting part of a plant and inducing it to sprout roots. The result is an "own-root" plant, as opposed to those plants that do not grow on roots of their own but are joined to the roots of another species. Hybrid tea roses do not grow well on their own roots, but if you choose a good climber (or, in a warm climate, a tea rose), you stand a good chance of getting offspring that grow and bloom quite well.

Cuttings taken while the parent plant is growing, usually in June or early July, are known as softwood cuttings. Hardwood cuttings are taken from a dormant plant, either in the late fall or the early spring. Cuttings may be rooted in several ways, but one that has worked particularly well for me is shown in the series of drawings at the right.

Once plants have started, many gardeners in cold climates transfer the young bushes to the protection of a cold frame, hotbed or greenhouse, where they stay through the first winter. Bushes moved at once into the garden should be carefully protected against winter weather by the hilling method (page 61).

SOIL LAYERING   New plants can also be propagated by a practice known as layering, in which stems are induced to take root while they are still attached to—and nourished by—the parent plant. Of the several methods of layering used, the most satisfactory is the one called soil layering. It works best on climbers having flexible arching canes, for the cane that is to be rooted must be bent over so that part of it can be buried in the ground. How this technique can be applied is detailed in the drawings that appear on page 90.

BUDDING   The most difficult and time-consuming method of propagating plants vegetatively is budding, which is now used to reproduce nearly all commercial rose plants, especially hybrid varieties. In this process a sliver of stem bearing a bud eye (page 10) of the desired variety is inserted beneath the bark of another species of rose known to have especially vigorous roots. Most amateur rose growers are willing to leave this technique to nurserymen; it is far easier to buy strong plants and set them in the garden and enjoy their blooms than it is to go through the process of growing them from scratch. For one thing, the production of Number 1 grade rose plants takes two growing seasons in a nursery—about half a year for the rootstock plants to develop strong roots and a year and a half more for the cultivated flowering varieties to grow from single buds to full-sized plants. But there is nothing arcane about the procedure, and only patient practice is necessary to develop the mechanical skills that the professionals use.

The rootstock upon which the flower-bearing varieties are budded is usually a cultivated type of wild rose, but this is not always the case. The roses most commonly used are the wild rose

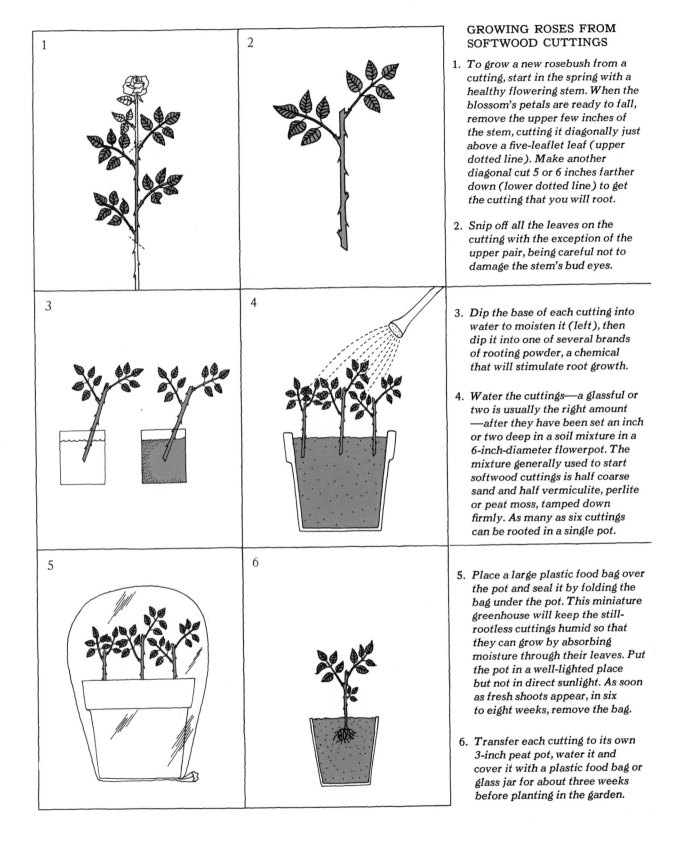

GROWING ROSES FROM SOFTWOOD CUTTINGS

1. *To grow a new rosebush from a cutting, start in the spring with a healthy flowering stem. When the blossom's petals are ready to fall, remove the upper few inches of the stem, cutting it diagonally just above a five-leaflet leaf (upper dotted line). Make another diagonal cut 5 or 6 inches farther down (lower dotted line) to get the cutting that you will root.*

2. *Snip off all the leaves on the cutting with the exception of the upper pair, being careful not to damage the stem's bud eyes.*

3. *Dip the base of each cutting into water to moisten it (left), then dip it into one of several brands of rooting powder, a chemical that will stimulate root growth.*

4. *Water the cuttings—a glassful or two is usually the right amount —after they have been set an inch or two deep in a soil mixture in a 6-inch-diameter flowerpot. The mixture generally used to start softwood cuttings is half coarse sand and half vermiculite, perlite or peat moss, tamped down firmly. As many as six cuttings can be rooted in a single pot.*

5. *Place a large plastic food bag over the pot and seal it by folding the bag under the pot. This miniature greenhouse will keep the still-rootless cuttings humid so that they can grow by absorbing moisture through their leaves. Put the pot in a well-lighted place but not in direct sunlight. As soon as fresh shoots appear, in six to eight weeks, remove the bag.*

6. *Transfer each cutting to its own 3-inch peat pot, water it and cover it with a plastic food bag or glass jar for about three weeks before planting in the garden.*

GROWING A NEW ROSE PLANT FROM A CANE

1. *A rosebush with flexible canes can generate a new plant by "soil layering"—roots sprout from a cane partly buried in a 7- or 8-inch hole in spring or early summer. Note the point on the cane where it will be buried deepest, about a foot from its tip.*

2. *At the section to be buried deepest, make a shallow cut just below a bud eye (arrow). Put a matchstick in the cut to keep it open. Strip off the leaves on either side, moisten the cut and brush rooting powder into it.*

3. *A forked stick or crossed stakes placed just below the cut (arrow) and a stone set on top hold the cane in place in the hole, which is filled with a half-and-half mixture of sand and either peat moss or vermiculite. Another stone is used to prop up the tip of the cane where it emerges from the ground.*

4. *By fall, a new root system will have developed in the area of the cut. To enable the tender new roots to survive the winter, however, the buried cane should be left attached to the parent plant until the following spring.*

5. *The next spring, while the new plant is still leafless, sever it from its parent (dotted line, right). Remove the soil above the plant and trim off the cane end near the new roots (dotted line, left).*

6. *After you have prepared a hole for transplanting, lift out the baby plant on a shovel, digging at least 8 inches behind the severed cane end to avoid cutting the roots. Steady the plant with a hand to keep the ball of soil around its roots intact and transfer it to the new hole, setting it so the top of its soil ball is at ground level.*

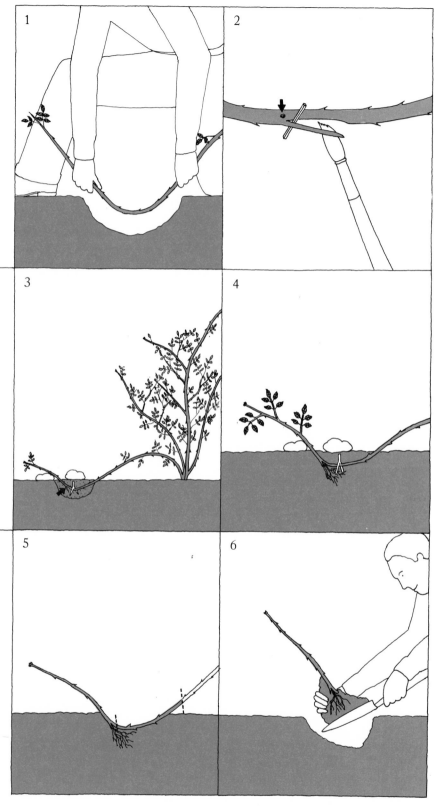

Rosa multiflora and a garden variety, the climber Dr. Huey. They root easily, have extremely vigorous root systems, are compatible with cultivated varieties of roses and seldom sprout suckers.

The rootstock must be prepared first. Nurserymen use 8- to 9-inch pieces of stems, from which all but the top two buds have been carefully removed, planting the pieces in late fall or late winter by simply inserting them about 3 inches into the ground in nursery rows. They are given a good watering, and soon form roots. That spring and summer, when the rootstock bushes have established themselves, the "budders"—the workers who insert the buds of the desirable hybrids into the stems of the root plants—go into the fields. They begin by wiping a section of the root plant's stem close to the ground and making a T-shaped cut in the bark there. Then they peel away the edges of the bark and insert a hybrid bud. This bud union is then wrapped, usually with a special rubber band that deteriorates after a few weeks, but holds the bud tightly to the rootstock long enough for the two to grow together.

At this point each plant consists of roots, the rootstock's own stem and the budded-on hybrid section. The growing stalk that has arisen from the bud is pruned if necessary to force it to make a number of branches. The following spring the rootstock stem is cut away, leaving a bush that has roots of one type and flower-bearing canes of another. If you would like to try your hand at budding, a simplified procedure is shown in the drawings on page 92.

Sooner or later almost every gardener who starts propagating his own plants is tempted to take the next step—rose breeding. For what rose lover does not carry within his heart a secret desire to create a new and better variety, one more lovely than any other ever grown? Perhaps he dreams of fame and fortune and even goes so far as to pick a name for his unknown beauty. The chance of his achieving this goal is very slim, for the most gifted of professional plant breeders rarely finds one rose out of ten thousand seedlings that is worth introducing into commerce.

However, the amateur should not be discouraged by the odds against commercial success. The techniques are simple, and even if the plants he creates are never grown outside of his own garden, he is still likely to enjoy them more than the loveliest varieties hybridized by other men. The professionals themselves are the first to say that rose breeding is a fascinating game of chance.

Because the genetic heritage of each rose is so complex, any seed—indeed, any growing bush—may produce flowers or growth characteristics that were unknown before. It is possible for the genes in a plant or even part of a plant to undergo a sudden change—a mutation—and grow differently than its progenitors did. The mu-

CREATING NEW ROSES

HOW TO GRAFT A ROSE ONTO STURDY ROOTS

1. *To strengthen a delicate hybrid rose, it is usually grafted, or "budded," to the rootstock of a more robust variety. In midseason cut a "bud stick," a 4- to 5-inch section of mature cane, from the hybrid rose and remove its thorns and leaves (left).*

2. *With a sharp knife, make an inch-long, T-shaped incision (dotted lines) through the bark—no deeper—at the base of the rose that has been selected as the rootstock. The top of the T should reach halfway around the cane.*

3. *Holding the trimmed bud stick as shown, remove a ¾-inch-long slice of bark containing a healthy bud. To avoid damaging the bud, cut deep enough to include a sliver of wood with the bark. Peel the wood away from the bud as indicated by the arrow in the inset.*

4. *After laying open the flaps cut in the rootstock, insert the piece of bark into the incision, bud side outward. Trim the bark so that it will make firm contact with the exposed wood of the rootstock. Then press the flaps around the bud, closing the incision.*

5. *Bind up the graft with a wide rubber band, or with the special material called rubber budding band that can be bought at garden stores. Wind carefully above and below the bud in both directions.*

6. *The completed bud graft should look like this. If the graft has taken, the bud will continue to remain green; in a week or 10 days it will begin to swell, and by the end of the season it will have become a full-fledged cane. The following spring, prune the rootstock back to a point ½ inch above the graft, or "bud union."*

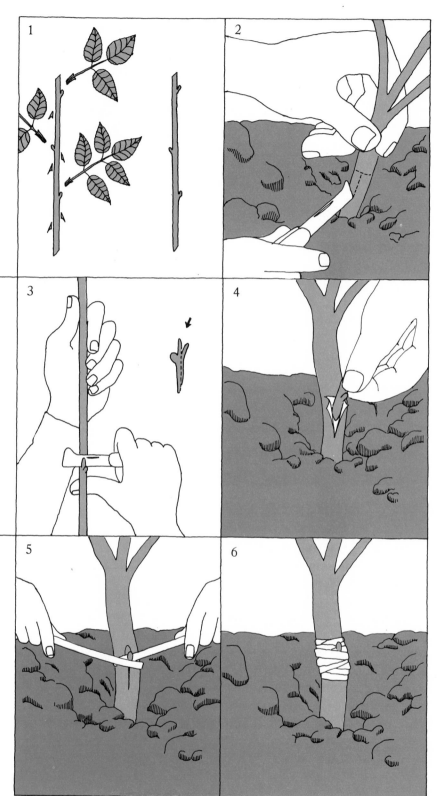

tant, or "sport," can be preserved and propagated simply by taking cuttings from it. A recent example is the New Dawn rose, a continuously blooming climber that was awarded the first U.S. plant patent. New Dawn was discovered as a mutant branch on a bush of a Dr. W. Van Fleet rose, a type that blooms once a season.

Mutants occur only rarely and at unpredictable times, however. Most new rose varieties are created by growing plants from seeds. Even then, the results may be surprising—outright failures, exotic throwbacks to some obscure ancestor, or fabulous triumphs. Indeed there is no better proof of the importance of luck than the incredible success of the great rose breeder Eugene Boerner, who produced two all-time favorite roses, Vogue and Fashion, each unique, from two seeds that came out of the same seed pod.

An outstanding example of what an amateur can achieve in the field of hybridization is the hybrid tea rose shown on the cover of this book. Named the Lady Bird Johnson and introduced commercially in the fall of 1970, this orange-red beauty was bred by Eldon C. Curtis, a Dallas, Texas, insurance salesman who had begun breeding roses as a hobby in 1960 (his very first batch of seedlings produced a new hybrid tea, Miss Hillcrest). Curtis crossed two orange roses, using the vigorously growing Montezuma as the female parent, and the colorful, fragrant Hawaii as the male parent. After planting the seeds in the back yard of his suburban home, he got a seedling that, growing on its own roots, produced interesting-looking buds. But the buds refused to open.

Curtis was on the verge of scrapping the plant, but E. V. Kimbrew, a professional rose grower, thought that the results were promising enough to be carried a step further. Kimbrew took budwood from the plant for test-growing in his fields.

He did not attempt to grow the cuttings on roots of their own, but budded them onto the stronger roots of multiflora roses. Grown this way, plants of the new variety put forth long, urn-shaped buds —and wide-opening flowers of exceptional form and substance. Excited by the blooms, Kimbrew showed them to Dr. Eldon Lyle, plant pathologist and director of the Texas Rose Research Foundation. Dr. Lyle had the happy idea of making the variety an all-Texas affair by naming it after a famous fellow Texan then residing in the White House, Mrs. Lyndon Johnson. The First Lady quickly agreed to have it as her namesake.

Although every amateur cannot expect Curtis' success, anyone can use the same techniques he employs. The simplest way to create a new kind of rose is to pick a ripe seed pod, or hip, from a bush, plant the fertile seeds and grow the new bushes to maturity. Each is likely to be quite different from the other—and from the bush that bore the seed pod. There is no way to tell what the results will be until the plants flower; even the character of the flower that produced the seed pod is a poor guide for predicting the outcome. This flower provided the female seed but it may or may not have provided the male pollen to fertilize the seeds. With this method only the female of the new plant's parents can be selected, and the chances of creating an improved rose are very small.

Despite the unfavorable odds, such half-controlled breeding was practiced with remarkable success over the centuries in Oriental and European gardens—presumably the lovely tea roses, gallicas, damasks and hundreds of others were created in this way. But a much more effective breeding technique was developed by the Empress Josephine's gardeners at Malmaison. They pioneered controlled pollination, in which the seeds of a selected flower are artificially fertilized with pollen specifically gathered for the purpose. In this way both of a new rose's parents can be selected, and it becomes much easier to breed for desirable characteristics.

Controlled pollination has led to the marvelous rose varieties now in commerce—such a wide choice an amateur may rightfully ask himself how he can possibly hope to develop a rose that possesses greater qualities than those already on the market. Yet some roses are susceptible to disease; others lack hardiness; certain ones blossom abundantly only once during a season, and, all too often, some roses with truly lovely flowers fail to have attractive foliage or thrifty growth habits. And despite the great assortment of colors among roses—which include everything from the palest white to a purplish red so dark it appears almost black—there are some hues that have never been grown. Blue, for example, is missing from the rose spectrum (although there are lavender and purple roses).

The quest for a blue rose has long intrigued—and frustrated—breeders and rose gardeners alike. In 1955, just such a plant was advertised by an enterprising con man in St. Louis, Missouri. But thousands of buyers soon learned to their dismay that his so-called blue rose was merely a red variety whose blooms took on a bluish cast only as they died; the charlatan was eventually jailed for using the mails to defraud. Honest efforts to develop a truly blue rose have not been successful to date.

Still, the professional hybridizers keep trying, and one—Mrs. Dorothy Whisler of Shafter, California—has obtained some encouraging results. Using sophisticated techniques of chemical analysis, Mrs. Whisler selected the crossbred lavender hybrid teas in order to produce offspring having optimum amounts of cyanidin, the pigment that imparts purple or magenta tones, and flavone, the pigment that gives light yellow tones. In 1960, she crossed two lilac-colored roses, Simone (page 39) and Sterling Silver, and three years later she bred a seedling from this cross to a silvery lavender

Song of Paris rose. The second cross produced a rose with a distinctly bluish tone, which Mrs. Whisler compared to the blue haze over a mountain and named Blue Heaven. Mrs. Whisler does not claim that Blue Heaven is really blue; indeed she doubts that a true blue rose will ever be developed. However, she herself may make further progress toward that goal by crossbreeding to her Blue Heaven. It is also possible that a natural mutation may produce a blue rose, or that the color may be artificially introduced by altering the genes of rose seeds with X-rays, atomic radiation or certain chemicals.

Most amateurs, of course, do not even consider such complex methods. They simply cross two plants in their garden and hope that they will get seeds. Sometimes they do and sometimes they don't. One reason for failure is that all roses will not cross with one another. This roadblock to rose breeding is found inside the plant cells. The cells of all roses do not have the same number of chromosomes, the groups of genetic units that transmit hereditary characteristics. Most modern roses have either 14 or 28 chromosomes. Plants with like numbers cross readily, but those with unlike numbers are difficult to cross.

The actual pollination of roses consists simply of transferring pollen, which looks like yellow or orange dust, from the anthers, or male organs, of a flower to the pistils, or female organs, of a flower (*page 11*). When two different varieties of roses are used as parents, the technique is called cross-pollination. When the pollen of a flower is applied to the pistils of another flower of the same variety, the result is self-pollination.

The process of preparing a rose flower to serve as the seed, or female, parent begins a few hours to a day before the flower is due to open, while the pollen grains are still immature and the petals are still covering the sex organs. The flower petals are first cut away with small scissors or pulled off with the fingers (*page 97*); the sepals, the green leaflike petals beneath the colored petals, may be cut away or peeled back. Then the male parts of the blossoms, the fine anthers, are picked off with tweezers. The flower now has only its female parts, the pistils, left in its center. The blossom should then be covered with a bag to keep out pollen that might be carried by insects or wind. Now its seeds cannot be fertilized except by pollen deliberately provided.

In a day or two the fuzzy stigma, looking like a miniature tuft of golden carpet atop the female pistils, will become sticky and be ready to receive pollen. At that time ripe pollen from the male parent should be applied to the stigmas. The pollen is ripe when the flower anthers split open so that the pollen inside can be seen to look like gold dust; ripening usually occurs about a day after the

THE GREEN "MONSTER"
What can happen as a result of chance mutation was startlingly illustrated in the early 19th Century with the appearance in America of Rosa chinensis viridiflora—an all-green rose (page 138). An occidental offshoot of a China rose, it is a free-flowering and otherwise normal plant, except that all its petals have been transformed into sepals, whorls of narrow, bronze-tinted green leaves that turn reddish brown with age; the flower, moreover, is completely sterile, having no stamens or pistils at all. Some gardeners see in it a strange kind of beauty, whereas others think that it merits its alternate Latin name, Rosa monstrosa, the monstrous rose.

rose is cut. For the amateur the simplest way to transfer pollen is to brush the anthers of the male flower over the stigmas of the female. Professional breeders collect the pollen in a dish and transfer it with a camel's-hair brush, but it is said that Francis Meilland, the French rose breeder who created the Peace rose, simply used the end of his finger.

After pollination the bag is replaced and left on for several weeks. If the cross has failed, the green hip at the base of the female flower will soon start to wither, and will eventually fall off. If the cross has taken, the hip will begin to grow. After four to six months, it will ripen and change color, usually to a cherry red, a bright yellow or a shiny orange. Then it can be picked and cut open so that the seeds inside can be picked out.

SELECTING SEEDS   The seeds are put in water, and any that are light enough to float should be discarded, for their lightness indicates that they are hollow and probably will not germinate. The plump remaining seeds are planted, 1 inch apart and about ¼ of an inch deep, in a flat filled with an equal mixture of sand, soil and peat moss. Each flat, with its contents identified by parental names, should then be placed in a refrigerator—its normal temperature of about 40° encourages seeds to germinate—and kept there for three months. After that the flat should be moved to a bright, sunny window in a room maintained at 65° to 70°. Some of the seeds will sprout tiny, oval leaves within two to three weeks, although most will take much longer; rose seeds have been known to lie dormant for as long as seven years, but most breeders discard seeds after eight months, accepting plants that germinate and forgetting those that do not.

With careful watering, the tiny seedlings grow quickly. When a seedling has three true leaves (not counting the tiny seed leaves) it should be transplanted into its own labeled pot. To the surprise of most amateur breeders, the first flowers often appear when young plants are only 4 to 5 inches tall. These first flowers do not indicate the size or form of the blossoms that will be produced by the mature bush, but will reveal the color of the new variety.

By the following spring, the young plants have reached a stage that usually separates the expert hybridizers from the beginners. The professionals select the promising seedlings, and bud them on the rootstocks of hardier varieties. Within a relatively short time, the plants come into blossom, giving full-sized flowers, from which the professional can then readily judge their value. But for most amateur breeders, it is rewarding enough to transplant the new rose plants into the garden to grow as they are, nourished by their own roots. If those first flowers bore a hint of blue, who knows what might one day come of yet another crossbreeding.

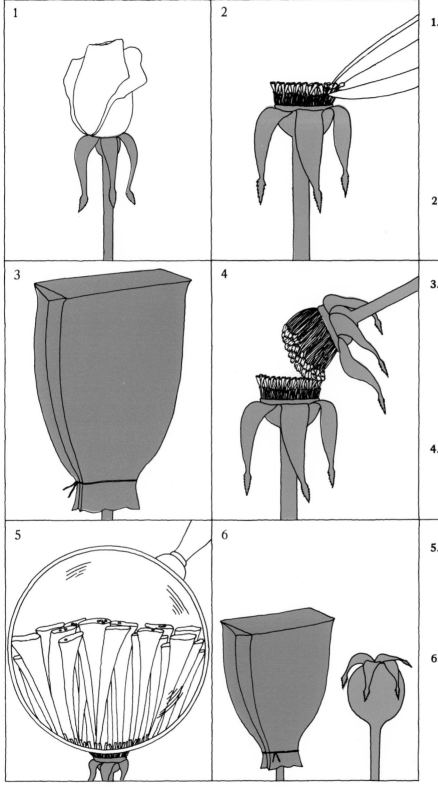

CROSSING ROSES

1. *To create your own new roses through hybridization, select blossoms from two varieties of plants when their petals are just starting to unfold, as in this drawing. Designate either bud as the female parent and the other as the male parent. Cut the male bud, taking a 6-inch stem, and put it in water. Then gently pull off all the petals from the female bud, starting with the outer row.*

2. *Using a magnifying glass and a tweezers, pull off the female parent's male stamens to keep the flower from pollinating itself.*

3. *Tie a small paper bag over the stripped bud to prevent the exposed female pistils from being fertilized by insect-borne pollen. After a day, remove the bag from the female flower and check the pistils with the magnifying glass. By this time they should have become slightly sticky on top, indicating that the female flower is ready to receive pollen.*

4. *When the male parent's anthers have begun to release pollen, visible through the magnifying glass, carefully rub the anthers over the female flower's pistils.*

5. *Using the magnifying glass, check to make certain that at least two or three yellow- or orange-colored grains of pollen are resting on top of the pistils, ready to fertilize the female flower. If no pollen grains are visible, repeat step 4.*

6. *Place the bag over the female flower again, removing it after a week. If pollination has occurred, the flower's round base, or hip, will have begun to swell (right). The ovules, or eggs, in the hip will take several months to mature, at which time they can be removed for later planting (page 95).*

A bouquet of arrangements

From a single flower to a massed display of blooms, roses can provide beauty in a variety of arrangements and surroundings. Alone or combined with other flowers, they can be casual or formal, intimate or elegant, riotous or restrained. One thing roses seldom are, however, is long lasting; without care their beauty tends to be sweet but fleeting. To make roses last as cut flowers they must be picked while still in the budding stage, then plunged immediately into several inches of tepid water, preferably water that contains one of the cut-flower preservatives sold by florists and garden supply stores. These chemical compounds, containing both nutrients and antibacterial agents, can double the life of a rose arrangement. Stand the roses in a cool place for at least an hour to cut down the process of transpiration—the loss of moisture through petals and foliage. Then, just before arranging them, cut off any unwanted foliage and strip off all leaves that would fall below the water surface, where they might rot and foul the water. A special stripping tool facilitates this task and also removes another troublesome appendage: thorns. Trim off a fraction of an inch of stem to open a fresh water-absorbing surface, and place the rose in the container. To hold it in place use a commercial flower holder—such as a block of foam plastic or a needlepoint holder—or force a ball of crumpled chicken wire into the mouth of the container.

The fundamental rules for arranging roses are like those for any flowers. Do not crowd the container; do not allow flowers to rest against one another, lest the movement of one dislodge the whole arrangement; and keep the composition in balance by putting darker colored flowers and more open buds toward the bottom, lighter colors and tighter buds toward the top. If the composition will be seen from several angles, circle the arrangement to make sure that it looks well from all sides —or do the arranging on a Lazy Susan. The character of the design itself *(following pages)* is best determined by the setting, the simplicity or elegance of the container—and the mood and tastes of the person who is doing the arranging.

A perfect Tropicana rose requires no arranging, except to be placed in an ideal container for it, a crystal bud vase.

Elegant formality

When the furnishings of a room are traditional in style, roses generally look best in an arrangement that reflects the quiet dignity of their surroundings. Colors that harmonize and blend into one another are better than sharp contrasts, and a good choice for a container is a footed vase or urn that lifts the flowers above the surface on which they stand. When foliage seems called for, choose one that is ornamental in form—like spiral eucalyptus *(below)*.

On a table in front of a low-keyed French painting, an open and deliberately simple arrangement of Queen Elizabeth and Regal Gold roses in a china shell creates an island of serenity in an object-filled environment.

The glory of red and pink roses, arranged in a bronze urn in combination with eucalyptus leaves, is reflected outward from the mirror on the wall. The bouquet was designed with this repeated exposure in mind.

A painted garland of roses on a Sèvres china vase established the theme for a classic arrangement of roses, salvia and delphiniums—except that the roses are the modern hybrid floribunda, Bridal Pink.

Four kinds of roses—red, pink, yellow and white—are combined with salvia in a bouquet designed for a terrace table. The gracefully curving salvia reiterates the diagonal pattern of the woven metal basket.

Easy informality

When roses are used for decorating informal settings—a porch, a patio, a sunroom—color combinations can be bolder and brighter and a more varied choice of flowers can be used with them. But in one respect casual rose arrangements require special care. They are more likely to be placed in locations where they will be seen in the round. For this reason they should be designed to look well from any direction one happens to approach them.

An exuberant bouquet for a sunny room that looks out over a garden combines pink and yellow roses with a multicolored array of other flowers—snapdragons, petunias and delphiniums—all contained in a glass vase.

In an oval pewter bucket rimmed with brass, delicate white roses with ruffled petals share the limelight with a new and unusual arrival in the horticultural world, a zinnia especially bred to produce light green flowers.

A cornucopia of full-blown roses, in shades of pink, yellow and white, spills from an antique Meissen bowl to brighten a

dark-paneled dining room. The white flowers scattered among the roses to blend them are gypsophila, or baby's breath.

An illustrated encyclopedia of roses 4

To help you choose from among the 5,000 or so different kinds of roses that are commercially available today, the following pages offer descriptions of 344 outstanding varieties. Any selection of roses is necessarily arbitrary, subject not only to personal tastes but also to the changes that come with time; new varieties are constantly being introduced, pushing many fine older roses out of growers' catalogues. The roses listed here, however, have proved themselves worthy and, with the exception of some of the older varieties, are believed to be generally available. Among the listings are some 50 All-America Rose Selections, a distinction bestowed upon a few roses each year by a nonprofit rose-testing organization.

General characteristics of each of the nine broad classes of roses are followed by detailed information about the selected varieties, including any exceptional characteristics such as an unusual number of petals or striking foliage. The characteristics and dimensions specified are based on plants grown under average conditions and given normal care; but even under ideal conditions sizes, colors and fragrance may vary widely.

The descriptions include some commonly used horticultural terms. A "single" blossom has one layer of five to seven fully formed petals; a "semidouble" has 10 to 20 in two or more layers; a "double" flower may have any number of petals over 20 in a rounded cluster. Varieties described as blooming "continuously" are not always fully covered with blossoms—they generally produce a big crop of flowers in spring and another in fall, with a steady but less profuse blooming in between. "Vigor" denotes general sturdiness of growth. "Hardiness" refers solely to a plant's cold resistance, "tenderness" to its lack of cold resistance. The introduction to each class of rose indicates in which climate zones most of the varieties in that class can be expected to be hardy without winter protection.

For quick reference, all the varieties of roses described here under their class headings are listed in a master alphabetical chart on pages 146-152, with their main characteristics and uses noted.

A portrait of rose varieties by Allianora Rosse groups polyanthas, older roses and a miniature around opulent modern hybrids, including the brilliant scarlet Mirandy and the famous yellow Peace.

AMERICAN HERITAGE   BEWITCHED

CHARLOTTE ARMSTRONG

Hybrid tea roses

Hybrid teas are the most widely grown roses today, even though as a type they are little more than a hundred years old. They owe their popularity to their amazing color range (notably including yellow shades, not so often found in other types), their long, strong stems, the size and elegance of their individual blossoms, the fragrance of many varieties, and their ability to bloom abundantly and almost continuously from spring until frost in Zones 3-8 and over a longer period in Zones 9-10 (page 153). Most varieties are hardy without winter protection in Zones 6-10 but should be protected in Zones 3-5 (page 61). Especially hardy varieties are noted in the entries below.

The most popular hybrid teas today have long, pointed buds and high-centered blooms. These characteristics, together with strong, straight stems, symmetrical leaves and crisp, long-lasting blossoms, make a good rose for exhibition. Many varieties that lack one or more of these traits are nevertheless good garden roses—i.e., vigorous, compact plants that provide plenty of flowers for cutting and require little upkeep. Every hybrid tea, whether for garden or show, should be grown in a bed reserved for roses alone.

Most hybrid teas bear double blossoms with 20 to 50 velvety or satin-textured petals; some have 70 or more. A few have single blossoms with five to seven petals; others are semidoubles with less than 20. The blossoms, some as large as 6 inches across, grow on bushes that range in height from 2 to as much as 6 feet if the plants are not cut back by pruning or severe winter damage. Colors include many shades of white, yellow, orange, pink, red, lavender and maroon; there are also blends and multicolors. Leaves are generally dark or medium green; in a few varieties new foliage is dark red before becoming green. The texture of the foliage ranges from glossy and leathery in some varieties to dull and almost paper thin in others. Most hybrid teas have fairly large thorns; a few relatively thornless varieties are noted below.

ALLEGRO. Profuse orange-red double blossoms are 3 to 4 inches across and have a slight fragrance. Plants grow more than 4 feet tall. Introduced 1962.

AMERICAN HERITAGE. This excellent exhibition rose has exceptionally long, pointed buds that open into high-centered flowers 3 to 5 inches across. The lushly doubled blooms have 50 to 60 petals each that are ivory at the base blending into salmon, with edges that turn darker as the flower ages. They have no fragrance. A compact, moderate-blooming bush 2½ to 4 feet tall. Introduced 1965. All-America Rose Selection 1966.

BEWITCHED. Large (3- to 5-inch), flat, double blossoms are a bright rose-pink and have a sweet, clovelike fragrance. Plants grow more than 4 feet tall. An excellent garden rose requiring minimum care. Introduced 1967. All-America Rose Selection 1967.

BLANCHE MALLERIN. A classic rose with beautifully formed buds that open into pure white double blossoms

3 to 4½ inches in diameter. Sweet fragrance. Plants grow 2½ to 4 feet tall, with few thorns. Introduced 1941.

BUCCANEER. Bright yellow double flowers are 3 to 4 inches across and have a moderate fragrance. Plants grow over 4 feet tall, with dark, leathery foliage. Introduced 1952. Classified as a grandiflora until 1971.

CANDY STRIPE. Very large double flowers, up to 6 inches across, are dusty pink with lighter pink and off-white stripes. Strong tealike fragrance. Blooms profusely in a well-shaped bush 2½ to 4 feet tall. Introduced 1963.

CHARLOTTE ARMSTRONG. This veteran show rose, winner of many gold metals and parent of many newer roses, has pointed, dark red buds that open into 3- to 5-inch double blossoms of deep pink. Moderate tea fragrance. Plants bloom profusely and are extremely vigorous, usually growing to a height of over 4 feet. Introduced 1940. All-America Rose Selection 1941.

CHICAGO PEACE. This profusely blooming mutation of the famous Peace rose produces elegantly shaped double flowers 4 to 6 inches across, of a pink-and-yellow blend with occasional copper tones. Slight fragrance. Grows in compact bushes, 2½ to 4 feet tall, having strong stems and glossy foliage. Introduced 1962.

CHRISTIAN DIOR. Abundant 3- to 4½-inch double flowers are crimson with scarlet shading and have a slight fragrance. Plants grow as upright bushes, 2½ to 4 feet tall, with dark, glossy foliage and few thorns. Introduced 1958. All-America Rose Selection 1962.

CHRISTOPHER STONE. Scarlet-crimson double flowers are 3 to 4 inches across. Sweet clove fragrance. Sprawling bushes grow 2½ to 4 feet tall. Among the earliest red hybrid teas still being grown. Introduced 1935.

CHRYSLER IMPERIAL. Long, pointed buds open to very high-centered 3- to 5-inch double flowers of dark crimson, with still darker red shadings. Strong fragrance. Blooms moderately on stiff, upright bushes, 2½ to 4 feet tall. Full, dark green foliage. An outstanding exhibition rose. Introduced 1952. All-America Rose Selection 1953.

COMMAND PERFORMANCE. Abundant semidouble blooms of show quality, 3 to 4 inches across, with fewer than 20 petals each, are orange red in color. Strong fragrance. An upright plant, over 4 feet tall, with thick sturdy canes. Introduced 1970. All-America Rose Selection 1971.

CONFIDENCE. Double blossoms of a delicate pink-and-yellow blend are 3 to 5 inches across and bloom profusely, with an average bush producing at least 40 or 50 flowers per season. Moderate fragrance. Plants grow 2½ to 4 feet tall. A favorite show rose. Introduced 1951.

CRIMSON GLORY. One of the finest of the red hybrid teas, Crimson Glory has velvety, deep crimson double blooms, 3 to 4 inches in diameter, and a strong clove fragrance. Plants reach a height of 2½ to 4 feet and have a graceful, spreading growth habit. Not a good parent for breeding purposes, but especially hardy. Introduced 1935.

DAINTY BESS. Generally considered the best of the hybrid tea singles, this variety bears a profusion of five-petaled single blossoms, 3 to 4 inches across, of a soft rose

CHRISTIAN DIOR   COMMAND PERFORMANCE

DAINTY BESS

FIRST PRIZE

KORDES' PERFECTA

pink with dark red stamens and fluted edges. Moderate fragrance; few thorns. Plants are vigorous and grow 2½ to 4 feet tall, with heavy foliage. A hardy garden rose, also successful as a show rose. Introduced 1925.

DAVE DAVIS. High-centered, dark red double flowers, 4 to 5 inches across, bloom continuously and profusely. Strong clove fragrance; leathery foliage; few thorns. Plants grow over 4 feet tall. Introduced 1964.

DR. BROWNELL. Abundant, large (4- to 5-inch) double flowers are buff with yellow centers. Strong fragrance. Plants grow 2½ to 4 feet tall, with dark, glossy foliage. Named after the famous amateur rose breeder Dr. W. A. Brownell. Introduced 1964.

ECLIPSE. Very long, pointed buds open into 3- to 5-inch, golden yellow double blossoms of show quality. Moderate fragrance. Vigorous and hardy, the plants grow 2½ to 4 feet tall and have long strong stems and full, leathery foliage. One of the finest yellow roses of any class, the variety owes its name to the fact that it first bloomed on the day of the eclipse of August 31, 1932. Introduced 1935.

ETOILE DE HOLLANDE. This free-flowering old favorite has bright red double blossoms 3 to 5 inches in diameter. Strong clove fragrance. Compact bushes grow 2½ to 4 feet tall and have soft green foliage. Introduced 1919.

FIRST PRIZE. Profuse, elegant and extremely large (4- to 6-inch) double blooms are deep rose with ivory centers and have a moderate fragrance. An upright, vigorously growing plant 2½ to 4 feet tall, with strong stems and handsome foliage. A fine show rose. Introduced 1970. All-America Rose Selection 1970.

FRAGRANT CLOUD (also called Duftwolke, Nuage Parfumé). Abundant coral-red double blooms are 4 to 5 inches in diameter, with a strong tea fragrance. Plants grow more than 4 feet tall. A good show rose and garden rose. Introduced 1968.

GARDEN PARTY. Pale yellow, 4- to 5-inch double blooms shade off to white with pink tinges. Colors deepen in fall. Slight fragrance. Plants are bushy, well branched and free blooming, and grow 2½ to 4 feet tall; leaves are dark green on top and reddish underneath. Introduced 1959. All-America Rose Selection 1960.

GOLDEN PRINCE. Rich yellow double blossoms, 3 to 5 inches across, have wide-opening petals. Slight fragrance; handsome, glossy foliage. Plants grow as compact bushes, 2½ to 4 feet tall. Introduced 1968.

HAWAII. Large (5- to 6-inch) double flowers are coral orange in color and have a heavy, raspberrylike fragrance. Plants grow in vigorous bushes 2½ to 4 feet tall. Introduced 1960.

KING'S RANSOM. Large, elegant, golden yellow double flowers 5 to 6 inches across have a moderate fragrance and bloom rather sparsely on a compact bush that grows over 4 feet tall. Glossy foliage. Not very hardy, but a good show rose for growing in moderate climates. Introduced 1961. All-America Rose Selection 1962.

KORDES' PERFECTA (also called Perfecta). Buds that are shaped like urns open into 4- to 5-inch double blossoms of a deep pink and yellow blend, with 65 or 70 petals each. Colors deepen in hot weather, with dark streaks on outer petals. Strong tea fragrance. Grows as a compact, hardy, free-blooming bush, 2½ to 4 feet tall, with stiff stems and dark, glossy foliage. Bred by the famous German hybridizer Wilhelm Kordes. Introduced 1957.

LAURA. Abundant salmon and coral-pink double flowers are 4 to 5 inches in diameter and have a moderate fragrance. Upright, vigorous bushes grow over 4 feet tall, with foliage that turns from reddish green to medium green as it matures. Introduced 1969.

LUCKY PIECE. This offspring of the Peace rose closely resembles its parent, but has blossoms of a darker blend of gold, pink and copper. Bears abundant 5- to 6-inch double flowers of show quality and has a moderate fragrance. Grows as a vigorous, compact, hardy bush 2½ to 4 feet tall, with full, glossy foliage. Introduced 1962.

MATTERHORN. Many well-shaped, ivory white double flowers, 3 to 5 inches across, grow on exceptionally tall bushes, almost always over 4 feet high, and sometimes considerably higher. Slight fragrance. Introduced 1965. All-America Rose Selection 1966.

MIRANDY. Deep red double flowers, 4 to 6 inches across, have a heavy, spicy clove fragrance. Compact, bushy plants grow 2½ to 4 feet tall and have leathery foliage. Introduced 1945. All-America Rose Selection 1945.

MISS ALL-AMERICAN BEAUTY (also called Maria Callas). Well-shaped, long-lasting double flowers of a vivid deep pink color are 4 to 5 inches across and bloom profusely and continuously. Strong tea fragrance. Grows as a vigorous, hardy bush over 4 feet tall with long strong stems and full, disease-resistant foliage. A superb variety. Introduced 1965. All-America Rose Selection 1968.

MISTER LINCOLN. Vigorous bushes produce a moderate number of large, show-quality double blossoms, dark red in color and up to 6 inches in diameter. Strong fragrance. Plants grow more than 4 feet tall with reddish stems and full dark foliage. Introduced 1964. All-America Rose Selection 1965.

MOJAVE. Well-shaped double blooms, 3½ to 4½ inches across, are much favored by flower arrangers for their unusual apricot-orange color and prominent veins. Slight fragrance. Plants grow as vigorous, upright bushes 2½ to 4 feet tall, with long stems and few thorns. Buds are long and delicately shaped. Introduced 1954. All-America Rose Selection 1954.

OKLAHOMA. One of the darkest red hybrid teas, Oklahoma bears show-quality double blossoms 4 to 5½ inches across. Strong tea fragrance. Well-branched bushes 2½ to 4 feet tall, with dark, glossy foliage. Introduced 1964.

PASCALI. Creamy white double blossoms, 3 to 4 inches across, bloom profusely and have a slight fragrance. Bushes grow vigorously over 4 feet tall, with dark green foliage and few thorns. A good exhibition rose. Introduced 1963. All-America Rose Slection 1969.

PEACE (also called Gioia, Gloria Dei, Mme. A. Meilland). Classic pointed buds open slowly into 5- to 6-inch double flowers, golden yellow at the base with rose-pink

MISTER LINCOLN

PEACE

ROYAL HIGHNESS

TIFFANY

WHITE WINGS

edging that deepens and spreads as the petals unfold. Slight fragrance. Vigorous, hardy, bushy plants grow over 4 feet tall, with long, sturdy stems and large, dark, leathery, disease-resistant leaves. Considered by many the greatest rose ever bred, Peace was bred in France by the famous hybridizer Francis Meilland and introduced in America in 1945. All-America Rose Selection 1946.

PHARAOH (also called Pharaon). Pointed, dark maroon buds open into 4- to 5-inch double flowers of a bright orange red with golden stamens. Moderate fragrance. Plants are free-flowering and grow 2½ to 4 feet tall on stiff stems. Foliage is especially handsome, bronze colored when young, turning bright green as it matures. A successful show rose. Introduced 1967.

ROYAL HIGHNESS. Abundant, high-centered, light pink double blossoms are 4½ to 5½ inches in diameter and have a strong tea fragrance. Plants grow as upright, well-proportioned bushes 2½ to 4 feet tall with rich, glossy foliage. Introduced 1962. All-America Rose Selection 1963.

SUTTER'S GOLD. Orange buds overlaid with red open into golden orange double flowers 4 to 5 inches in diameter. Strong, fruity fragrance. Bushes grow 2½ to 4 feet tall, with few thorns and attractive but somewhat sparse foliage. Does best in cool climates. Introduced 1950. All-America Rose Selection 1950.

SWARTHMORE. An extremely vigorous, free-blooming rose with good show form, Swarthmore bears rose-red double flowers, 3 to 5 inches in diameter, that have a slight fragrance. Plants are strong and grow over 4 feet tall, with dark foliage. Introduced 1963.

TIFFANY. Show-quality double flowers of a pink and gold blend, 4 to 5 inches in diameter, bloom profusely and have a strong fragrance. Plants are very vigorous and grow 2½ to 4 feet high, with full, light green foliage. Introduced 1954. All-America Rose Selection 1955.

TROPICANA (also called Super Star). Excellent for garden or show purposes, Tropicana produces many elegant, 4- to 5-inch double flowers of an intense coral-orange color. Strong fruity fragrance. Plants are exceptionally vigorous; they grow 2½ to 4 feet tall and have sturdy, very thorny stems and glossy, disease-resistant foliage. The blooms are long lasting and colorfast. Introduced 1962. All-America Rose Selection 1963.

WHITE KNIGHT. Long, pointed buds open into 3- to 4-inch double blossoms, with velvety petals that curl back sharply as they open wide. No fragrance. Upright bushes grow 2½ to 4 feet tall. A good white show rose. Introduced 1955. All-America Rose Selection 1958.

WHITE WINGS. Five-petaled single blossoms are 3 to 4 inches across, with white petals and chocolate-colored anthers, and appear in large clusters. Moderate fragrance. Plants grow 2½ to 4 feet tall. Introduced 1947.

Floribunda roses

Floribunda roses blossom almost continuously except for a short midwinter dormant period in Zones 9-10, and from spring until frost in Zones 3-8 *(page 153).* Combining the virtues of their parents—the hardy polyantha *(page 125)*, with its clusters of small blossoms, and the showy hybrid tea rose *(page 108)*, with its large blossoms on long stems—they produce clusters of moderately large blooms on fairly long stems, and are relatively hardy, most varieties surviving without winter protection in Zones 6-10.

Most varieties have elegant, high-centered, 2- to 4-inch blossoms, with long, pointed buds similar to those of hybrid teas. The blossoms are often heavily doubled, with up to 60 or more petals; there are also five-petaled single blossoms and semidoubles with fewer than 20 petals. Colors range from snowy white and cream to yellow, apricot, orange, coral, pink, red and lavender. Compact, well-shaped bushes usually grow 2 to 3 feet tall and wide and have foliage and thorns similar to but smaller than those of hybrid teas.

Floribundas make good hedges and can be massed in beds of their own or in front of taller roses. They provide constant color and good cut flowers.

ANGEL FACE. Double flowers, 3 to 4 inches across, have wavy, deep lavender petals. Strong, spicy fragrance. Plants grow less than 2 feet tall but bloom profusely. Introduced 1968. All-American Rose Selection 1969.

BETTY PRIOR. Five-petaled single flowers, 2 to 3 inches across, are medium pink in color and have a moderate fragrance. Betty Prior is among the tallest of the floribundas, reaching a height of 4 to 5 feet, and is exceptionally hardy and disease resistant. Considered one of the best of the older varieties. Introduced 1938.

BORDER GOLD. Lushly doubled flowers, 2 to 3½ inches across, bloom profusely in shades of medium to deep yellow. Slight fragrance; glossy foliage, dark bronze to green. Plants grow less than 2 feet tall. Introduced 1966.

CIRCUS. Double flowers of 45 to 58 petals each, 2 to 3 inches across, bloom in large clusters. Basic color is yellow, with many variations of pink, salmon and scarlet shadings. Moderate fragrance. Plants grow 2 to 3 feet tall. Introduced 1956. All-America Rose Selection 1956.

COLOR GIRL. Double flowers 2 to 3 inches across, in creamy white edged with deep pink, bloom in great abundance. Strong fragrance. Grows in compact bushes 2 to 3 feet tall. Introduced 1966.

DAGMAR SPÄTH (also called White Lafayette). Semidouble flowers, 2 to 3 inches across with fewer than 20 petals each, are white, edged with pink, and are borne in large clusters. Moderate fragrance. Plants grow 2 to 3 feet tall and are exceptionally hardy. Introduced 1936.

DREAM DUST. Small pink double flowers are 1 to 2 inches across and have a slight fragrance. Dark blue-green foliage. A compact and vigorous variety growing 2 to 3 feet tall. Introduced 1969.

ELIZABETH OF GLAMIS (also called Irish Beauty). Large double flowers, 3 to 4 inches across, are salmon pink in color and have a strong fragrance. Compact bushes grow 2 to 3 feet tall and bloom abundantly. Introduced 1964.

ELSE POULSEN (also called Joan Anderson). Bright pink, semidouble flowers, 1 to 2 inches across, have 10 pet-

ELSE POULSEN

EUROPEANA

GENE BOERNER

als and grow in large clusters. Slight fragrance; dark bronze foliage. Plants, which grow over 3 feet tall, make excellent hedges. One of the first floribundas, Else Poulsen was introduced in 1924.

EUROPEANA. Double flowers, 2 to 3 inches across, are crimson in color and bloom in large, heavy clusters that can be cut for use as long-lasting bouquets. Slight fragrance. Plants grow 2 to 3 feet tall. Introduced 1968. All-America Rose Selection 1968.

EUTIN. Dark red double flowers, 2 to 3 inches across, b'ossom in very large clusters on long, strong stems. Slight fragrance. Plants grow 2 to 3 feet tall and are exceptionally hardy and disease resistant. Introduced 1940.

FASHION. Double flowers, 2½ to 3½ inches across, are a distinctive blend of coral and peach pink. Moderate fragrance. Plants grow 2 to 3 feet tall. Introduced 1949. All-America Rose Selection 1950. Winner of many international awards.

FIRE KING. Double flowers, 1½ to 2½ inches across, are fiery scarlet in color and have a moderate fragrance. Plants are exceptionally vigorous and grow 3 feet tall and higher. Introduced 1958. All-America Rose Selection 1960.

FLORADORA. Bright orange-red double flowers, 1 to 2 inches across, grow in sprays of 6 to 12 blossoms that make attractive cuttings. Slight fragrance; globular buds. Plants grow 3 feet tall and higher. Introduced 1944. All-America Rose Selection 1945.

FRENSHAM. Semidouble flowers of 15 petals, 2 to 3 inches across, are a deep scarlet and have a slight fragrance. Plants, which grow 3 feet tall or more, are vigorous, bloom profusely and are notably thorny; they are frequently used as hedges and are exceptionally hardy and disease resistant. Introduced 1946.

GARNETTE. Small double flowers, 1 to 2 inches across, have 50 petals each, garnet red on top´and light yellow at the base. Slight fragrance; few thorns. Plants grow 2 to 3 feet tall. An excellent hothouse variety, Garnette is a favorite with florists for use in corsages as well as small arrangements. It also does well as a potted house plant. Introduced 1951.

GENE BOERNER. High-centered double flowers, 2½ to 3½ inches across, are vibrant pink and bloom profusely. Slight fragrance; few thorns. Plants grow 2 to 3 feet tall. Introduced 1968. All-America Rose Selection 1969.

GOLD CUP (also called Coupe d'Or). Double flowers, 3 to 4 inches across, are a deep golden yellow that fades slowly to white. Moderate fragrance; dark, glossy foliage. Plants grow 2 to 3 feet tall. Introduced 1957. All-America Rose Selection 1958.

GOLDEN CORONET. High-centered double flowers, 2 to 3 inches across, are chrome yellow. Slight fragrance, glossy foliage. Plants grow vigorously in compact bushes 2 to 3 feet tall. Introduced 1967.

GOLDILOCKS. Double flowers, 2½ to 3½ inches across, blossom deep yellow and gradually fade to a cream color. Moderate fragrance. Grows as a compact, bushy plant less than 2 feet tall. Introduced 1945.

ICEBERG (also called Schneewittchen, Fée des Neiges). Double flowers, 2½ to 4 inches in diameter, are white and open flat to reveal a hint of pink at the center. They have a strong fragrance and are among the tallest and most profusely blooming of the floribundas, reaching heights of 6 to 8 feet. They also have excellent disease resistance. Introduced 1958.

ICE WHITE (also called Vison Blanc). Pure white double flowers, 2 to 3 inches across, bloom profusely. Moderate fragrance; glossy foliage. Plants grow 3 feet tall or higher. Introduced 1966.

INDIAN GOLD. Double flowers, 2½ to 3½ inches across, are yellow with flushes of soft pink and blossom in large clusters on short stems. Moderate fragrance. Buds are flushed red. Plants grow as upright, compact bushes 2 to 3 feet tall. Introduced 1961.

IRISH MIST. Well-formed double flowers, 3½ to 4½ inches across, are orange salmon in color and bloom profusely. Slight fragrance; attractive dark foliage. Plants grow as dense bushes 2 to 3 feet tall. Introduced 1966.

IVORY FASHION. Large, 15-petaled semidouble flowers, 3½ to 4½ inches across, are ivory white in color and are shaped like wide, flat cups. Moderate fragrance. Plants grow 2 to 3 feet tall. Introduced 1958. All-America Rose Selection 1959.

JIMINY CRICKET. Double flowers, 2½ to 4 inches across, are a blend of coral orange and pink and have a moderate fragrance suggestive of rose geraniums. Buds are tangerine red. Plants grow 2 to 3 feet tall. Introduced 1954. All-America Rose Selection 1955.

LILAC CHARM. Five- to eight-petaled single flowers, 2½ to 4 inches across, are lilac with gold anthers and red filaments. Moderate fragrance. Grows in compact bushes 2 to 3 feet tall. Introduced 1962.

LITTLE DARLING. Double flowers, 1½ to 2½ inches across, are of a pink and yellow blend and bloom in great abundance. Moderate, spicy fragrance. Plants grow 3 feet tall or more. Introduced 1956.

MOUNTAIN HAZE. Double flowers of up to 60 petals each are 2 to 3 inches across and have lavender faces and silver undersides. Moderate fragrance; attractive dark foliage. Grows as a low, spreading bush less than 2 feet tall. Introduced 1967.

ORANGE CHIFFON. Double flowers, 2 to 3 inches across, have orange-salmon faces with undersides of silvery orange. No fragrance. Plants grow less than 2 feet tall but bloom profusely. Introduced 1966.

PINK BOUNTIFUL. Double flowers of up to 60 petals each, 2 to 3 inches across, are medium pink in color and have a moderate fragrance. Buds are short and pointed. Plants grow 2 to 3 feet tall. A popular variety among gardeners for perennial borders, and among florists as an all-season greenhouse rose. Introduced 1945.

PINOCCHIO (also called Rosenmärchen). Small, fully doubled flowers, 1 to 2 inches in diameter, are of a pink blend with deep pink edges. They bloom in long, attractive sprays and have a moderate fruity fragrance. Plants

JIMINY CRICKET

PINK BOUNTIFUL

ROSENELFE

SARATOGA

SPARTAN

grow 2 to 3 feet tall. Widely used for breeding, Pinocchio is a parent of Fashion and of a number of other excellent floribundas. Introduced 1942.

PRIDE OF NEWARK. Light pink double flowers, 3 to 4 inches across, bloom profusely on plants 2 to 3 feet tall. Strong fragrance; bronze-green foliage. Introduced 1966.

RED GLORY. Semidouble flowers of 10 to 12 petals each are 2½ to 3½ inches across and bloom in shades of red from cherry to rose. Slight fragrance. A prolific, continuous bloomer, Red Glory grows 3 feet tall and higher and makes an excellent hedge rose. Introduced 1958.

REDGOLD (also called Rouge et Or). Double flowers, 2 to 3 inches in diameter, are an unusual combination of chrome yellow with red at the edges. Slight fragrance. The plants grow 2 to 3 feet tall and bloom abundantly. Introduced 1971. All-America Rose Selection 1971.

RED PINOCCHIO. Velvety double flowers, 2 to 3 inches across, are dark red and have a moderate fragrance. Plants grow 2 to 3 feet tall and bloom profusely. Introduced 1947.

ROMAN HOLIDAY. Double flowers, 2 to 3 inches across, are of an unusually colorful blend with petals that are deep red at the edges and yellow at the base. Moderate fragrance. The plant's low growth, under 2 feet, and vivid coloration make it a popular choice for borders. Introduced 1966. All-America Rose Selection 1967.

ROSENELFE (also called Rose Elf). Medium pink double flowers, 1½ to 2½ inches across, bloom in clusters on long stems and are particularly suitable for cutting. Moderate fragrance. Plants grow vigorously as small bushes less than 2 feet tall. Introduced 1939.

RUMBA. Double flowers, 1½ to 2½ inches across, are of a red blend with a deeper red at the edges and lemon-yellow centers. Slight spicy fragrance. Plants grow 2 to 3 feet tall. Introduced 1960.

SARATOGA. Large, white, gardenia-shaped double flowers, 3½ to 4½ inches across, bloom profusely in irregular clusters. Strong fragrance. Plants grow 2 to 3 feet tall. Introduced 1963. All-America Rose Selection 1964.

SPARTAN (also called Sparte). Full, well-formed double flowers are 2½ to 3½ inches in diameter and are of an attractive orange-red blend. They have a strong fragrance. Plants grow over 3 feet tall. Introduced 1955. Winner of several gold medals.

SUNSPOT. Very large, abundant double flowers, 4 to 5 inches across, are of a butter-yellow color and have no fragrance. Plants grow 2 to 3 feet tall. One of the best yellow floribundas. Introduced 1965.

SWEET AND LOW. Small double flowers, 1 to 2 inches across, are salmon pink with lighter pink centers and bloom in large clusters. Slight fragrance. One of the smallest floribundas, growing only 12 to 15 inches high in compact bushes that make excellent borders. Introduced 1962.

VOGUE. Well-formed double flowers, 3½ to 4½ inches across, are pink and have a moderate fragrance. Plants grow more than 3 feet tall. Vogue was bred from the same combination that earlier produced Fashion. Introduced

1951. All-America Rose Selection 1952. Winner of several major awards.

WITCHING HOUR. Velvety double flowers, 2 to 3 inches across, are among the darkest of all red roses, appearing almost black. No fragrance. Blooms profusely on compact bushes 2 to 3 feet tall. Introduced 1967.

WORLD'S FAIR (also called Minna Kordes). Semidouble crimson flowers, 3 to 4 inches across, have prominent yellow stamens and a moderate spicy fragrance. Plants grow 2 to 3 feet tall. The variety was named in honor of the New York World's Fair of 1939-1940. Introduced 1939. All-America Rose Selection 1940.

Grandiflora roses

In the pursuit of elegant flowers, it was almost inevitable that rose breeders would combine the hardy, free-flowering floribundas *(page 112)* with the magnificently large-flowered, long-stemmed hybrid teas. In so doing, they created the Queen Elizabeth rose, which was introduced commercially in the United States in 1954 and became the basis for the newest type of rose, the grandiflora. (In great Britain, grandifloras are considered a subclass of the floribunda and are called floribundas, hybrid-tea type.)

Grandifloras combine the best qualities of their parents in blooming habit and hardiness, and flower continuously except for a brief midwinter dormancy in Zones 9-10, and from spring to frost in Zones 3-8 *(page 153)*. They bear great quantities of blossoms that are 3 to 5 inches in diameter—slightly smaller than most hybrid teas, slightly larger than floribundas. The blossoms are double, with as many as 60 petals, and may appear one to a stem or in candelabralike clusters on a bush; the stems of grandifloras are longer than those of floribundas. The buds and blossoms, as well as foliage and thorns, resemble those of hybrid teas. The grandifloras have a color range that is much the same as that of their parents: from white, pink, yellow and orange to dark red, but with no lavenders and few mixed colors. Oddly enough, while the blossom size and stem length of grandifloras are compromises between those of hybrid teas and floribundas, the height of grandifloras often outstrips that of both parents, and most varieties usually grow 3 to 6 or more feet high. This stature makes them ideal for use toward the back of a rose bed. Grandifloras also serve as lovely informal hedges and screens. And since even their clusters have long stems, all grandifloras are suitable for cutting.

ALASKA CENTENNIAL. Bears many dark scarlet double flowers, 3 to 5 inches across, with a moderate fragrance. Plants grow over 4 feet tall. Introduced 1967.

APRICOT NECTAR. Double flowers, 3½ to 4½ inches across, are apricot pink in color with a touch of gold at the base of the petals and have a strong, fruity fragrance. Not a tall plant, averaging 2 to 3 feet in height. Introduced as a floribunda in 1965, it was reclassified as a grandiflora in 1971. All-America Rose Selection 1966.

WORLD'S FAIR

APRICOT NECTAR

AQUARIUS   CARROUSEL

GRANADA

AQUARIUS. Large double flowers, 4 to 5 inches across, are light pink in color and have a moderate fragrance. Plants grow 4 feet tall or more and produce particularly fine roses for cutting. Introduced 1971. All-America Rose Selection 1971.

CAMELOT. Double flowers, 3½ to 4 inches across, are salmon pink in color and have a moderate, spicy fragrance. Leaves are glossy, dark and large. Plants grow vigorously from 2½ to 4 feet tall. Introduced 1964. All-America Rose Selection 1965.

CARROUSEL. Semidouble flowers, 3 to 4 inches across with about 20 petals each, are deep red in color and have a moderate fragrance. Leaves are large, dark and glossy. Plants grow 2½ to 4 feet tall and bloom profusely. Introduced 1950.

CHERRY GLOW. Double flowers, 3 to 4 inches across, are cherry red in color and have a moderate, spicy fragrance. Plants grow 2½ to 4 feet tall and bloom profusely. Introduced 1959.

COMANCHE. Double flowers, 3½ to 4½ inches across, are orange in color. Slight fragrance. Foliage is reddish bronze, becoming darker as the plant matures. Plants grow 4 feet tall and higher. Introduced 1968. All-America Rose Selection 1969.

DUET. Double flowers, 3 to 4 inches across, are rich pink with deeper pink undersides. Slight fragrance. The plants grow 2½ to 4 feet tall. Introduced as a hybrid tea in 1960, reclassified as a grandiflora in 1971. All-America Rose Selection 1961.

EL CAPITAN. Double flowers, 3½ to 4½ inches across, are medium red in color and bloom abundantly in small clusters. Slight fragrance. An upright, bushy plant over 4 feet tall. Introduced 1959.

GAY PRINCESS. Double flowers, 2 to 3 inches across, are light pink in color and have a moderate fragrance. Plants reach 2 to 3 feet in height and have few thorns. Originally introduced as a floribunda in 1967, Gay Princess was reclassified as a grandiflora in 1971. All-America Rose Selection 1967.

GOLDEN GIRL. Golden yellow double flowers, 3½ to 4½ inches across, blossom from long, slender buds. Moderate fragrance; light green foliage. An upright, tender plant that grows 2½ to 4 feet tall. Introduced 1959.

GOVERNOR MARK HATFIELD. Double flowers, 3½ to 4½ inches across, are dark red in color. Slight fragrance, pointed buds. Plants grow 4 feet tall and higher. Introduced 1962.

GRANADA. Double flowers, 3 to 5 inches across, are a blend of rose, red and yellow. Moderate fragrance, urn-shaped buds. Plants grow 2½ to 4 feet tall. Introduced in 1963 as a hybrid tea, and reclassified as a grandiflora in 1971. All-America Rose Selection 1964.

HECTOR DEANE. High-centered double flowers, 2 to 3½ inches across, are bright red with a trace of yellow at their bases. Strong, fruity scent. Plants grow 2½ to 4 feet tall. Introduced as a hybrid tea in 1938, reclassified as a grandiflora in 1971.

JANTZEN GIRL. Large crimson double flowers, 4 to 5 inches across with wavy petals, bloom abundantly in clusters. Slight fragrance. A tall plant, growing 4 feet tall and higher. Introduced 1961.

JOHN S. ARMSTRONG. Double flowers, 3 to 4 inches across, range from a medium red to dark red in color. Slight fragrance. Foliage is reddish when new. Plants grow 2½ to 4 feet tall and are very hardy. Introduced 1961. All-America Rose Selection 1962.

JUNE BRIDE. Double flowers 3 to 4 inches across, are creamy white in color and appear in clusters of three to seven. Moderate fragrance. Plants grow 4 feet tall and higher. Introduced 1957.

LUCKY LADY. Double flowers, 3½ to 4½ inches across, bloom in shades of light and darker pinks. Slight fragrance. Plants grow 2½ to 4 feet tall. Introduced 1966. All-America Rose Selection 1967.

MISS FRANCE (also called Pretty Girl). Double flowers, 3 to 4½ inches across, are scarlet in color and bloom profusely. Moderate fragrance. Plants grow vigorously, 2½ to 4 feet tall. Introduced as a hybrid tea in 1955 and subsequently reclassified as a grandiflora.

MONTEZUMA. Double flowers, 3 to 4 inches across, are orange red in color and open from short, shapely buds. Slight fragrance. Plants grow 2½ to 4 feet tall and are notably tender. Introduced 1955.

MOUNT SHASTA. Large white double flowers are 4 to 5 inches across and have a moderate fragrance. Foliage is gray-green and leathery. A tender plant, it grows over 4 feet tall. Introduced 1963.

OLÉ. Double flowers, 3 to 4 inches across, are orange red in color and have 45 to 55 crisp, ruffled petals each. Moderate fragrance. Plants grow 2½ to 4 feet tall and are tender. Introduced 1964.

PINK PARFAIT. Double flowers, 3 to 4 inches across, come in a blend of light pink colors. Slight fragrance. Plants grow 2½ to 4 feet tall. Introduced 1960. All-America Rose Selection 1961.

QUEEN ELIZABETH. Medium pink double flowers are 3 to 4 inches across and have a moderate fragrance. The original and most famous of the grandifloras, the Queen Elizabeth has long, almost thornless stems and is notably disease resistant and hardy. Plants grow over 4 feet high, often reaching 6 feet. Introduced 1954. All-America Rose Selection 1955. Winner of many gold medals.

QUEEN OF BERMUDA. Reddish orange double flowers are 3 to 4½ inches across and have a moderate fragrance. Plants grow vigorously, 2½ to 5 feet tall. Introduced 1956.

ROUNDELAY. Cardinal red double flowers, 3 to 4 inches across, bloom abundantly on plants 2½ to 4 feet tall. Moderate fragrance. Introduced 1954.

SAN ANTONIO. Double flowers, 3½ to 4½ inches across, are medium red to deep red in color. No fragrance. A tall, abundantly blooming variety, growing over 4 feet tall. Introduced 1967.

JOHN S. ARMSTRONG   PINK PARFAIT

QUEEN ELIZABETH

SCARLET KNIGHT (also called Samourai). Large double blossoms, 4 to 5 inches across, are a brilliant scarlet color. Slight fragrance. A big, upright, bushy plant that grows over 4 feet tall. Introduced 1966. All-America Rose Selection 1968.

STARFIRE. Large double flowers, 4 to 5 inches across and medium red in color, bloom in candelabralike clusters on long stems. Moderate fragrance; glossy foliage. Plants grow 2½ to 4 feet tall. Introduced 1958. All-America Rose Selection 1959.

STRAWBERRY BLONDE. Double flowers, 2½ to 3½ inches across, are light orange red in color and have a moderate, spicy fragrance. Plants bloom profusely and grow 2½ to 4 feet tall. Introduced 1966.

TROJAN. Large double flowers, 4 to 5 inches across, are pastel pink in color with yellow undersides. Moderate fragrance; leathery foliage. Plants bloom abundantly and grow 2½ to 4 feet tall. Introduced 1961.

Climbing roses

Climbing roses are not really climbing plants at all; if left in their natural state, they would soon bend under their own weight and sprawl along the ground. This is because their long canes do not have the tendrils or "holdfasts" with which true climbing plants, such as vines, hold onto upright structures. Climbing roses climb only if secured to supports.

Once properly secured, however, climbers are extremely versatile: they can be grown on arbors, along low fences or up walls. Allowed to creep or trail, they can cover an embankment while helping to keep its soil in place. In many varieties few blossoms appear the first year because the plants expend so much energy in their rapid growth.

Climbers comprise a wide variety of types. The most numerous are the large-flowered climbers, which bear 2- to 6-inch blossoms in loose clusters on strong, flexible canes 6 to 15 feet long. Most large-flowered climbers are hybrid descendants of wild climbers still found in various parts of the world. Modern varieties boast a wide range of colors and flower sizes. Some blossom heavily early in the season, producing few flowers later on; others follow their first crop of blossoms with intermittent bloom and then burst forth with another heavy crop in the fall. Large-flowered climbers are fairly resistant to disease and cold weather, and can generally grow without winter protection as far north as Zone 6 *(page 153)*.

Pillar roses, a subclass of the large-flowered climbers, do not grow as tall as other climbers, but stand more upright on stiffer canes to a height of 5 to 10 feet. They are often planted beside a post or pillar —hence their name—to which they are tied to prevent them from snapping in high winds.

Another distinct type of climber is the rambler. Its slender, supple canes grow very long (10 to 20 feet a year) and bear dense clusters of small flowers, each no more than 2 inches across. Most varieties bloom

SCARLET KNIGHT

once each year, in late spring or early summer, on canes that are one year old; a few flower again in the fall. Their colors are limited: deep red to weak pink. peach yellow and white; foliage is glossy. Though some types are susceptible to mildew *(pages 54-55)*, most true ramblers are extremely hardy, surviving subzero winters even when unprotected.

Climbing versions of hybrid tea roses, floribundas, grandifloras, polyanthas and even miniature roses are "sports," or chance mutations, of standard types. They are generally similar to the bush types from which they are descended—but their canes are considerably longer, and they are usually slightly less hardy and flower less profusely.

A strain of hybrids introduced in the 1950s by the noted breeder Wilhelm Kordes has been developed into a superb new class called *Kordesii*. Most of these climbers grow only 6 to 12 feet high, and are extremely hardy, requiring no winter protection as far north as Zone 4. They bloom profusely all season long, mostly in clusters and in the full range of rose colors.

AMERICAN PILLAR. Large-flowered climber. Five- to seven-petaled single flowers, 3 to 4 inches across, are of a red blend with white centers and blossom in clusters. No fragrance. Plants grow 15 to 20 feet tall and bloom in the spring. Introduced 1908.

BLAZE. Large-flowered climber. Semidouble flowers, 2 to 3 inches across with fewer than 20 petals each, are bright scarlet and bloom continuously. Slight fragrance. Plants grow 8 to 15 feet tall. Introduced 1932.

BLOSSOMTIME. Large-flowered climber. Clusters of double blossoms, 3 to 4 inches across, are of a pink blend and bloom continuously. Strong fragrance. A moderate climber that reaches a height of 6 to 10 feet. Introduced 1951.

CHEVY CHASE. Rambler. Dark crimson double flowers, 1½ to 2½ inches across, have 60 to 70 petals each and bloom in clusters on short stems in the spring. Moderate fragrance; soft, wrinkled, light green foliage. Plants grow to a height of 12 to 15 feet. Introduced 1939.

CLAIR MATIN. Large-flowered climber. Semidouble blossoms, 2 to 3 inches across with 12 to 18 petals each, are pink and bloom in rounded clusters almost continuously. Moderate fragrance; dark, leathery foliage. Plants reach heights of 12 feet. Introduced 1960.

CLIMBING CADENZA. Large-flowered climber. Dark red double blossoms, 2 to 3 inches across, bloom in spring and fall. Slight fragrance; glossy, dark, leathery foliage. Plants grow 8 to 12 feet tall. Introduced 1967.

CLIMBING CÉCILE BRUNNER. Climbing polyantha. A climbing version of the Sweetheart Rose, this variety has bright pink double blossoms, 1½ to 2½ inches across, with a moderate fragrance. Plants grow as tall as 20 feet or more and bloom in spring and fall. Introduced 1894.

CLIMBING CRIMSON GLORY. Climbing hybrid tea. Deep crimson double flowers, 3 to 4½ inches across, have a strong clove fragrance. Plants grow 8 to 12 feet tall and bloom in spring and fall. Introduced 1946.

BLAZE

CRIMSON GLORY

CLIMBING SHOT SILK

CLIMBING ETOILE DE HOLLANDE. Climbing hybrid tea. Bright red double flowers, 3 to 5 inches across, bloom profusely in spring and fall. Strong clove fragrance. Plants grow 10 to 20 feet tall. Introduced 1931.

CLIMBING MME. HENRI GUILLOT. Climbing hybrid tea. Double flowers, 3 to 5 inches across, are of a vivid orange-coral-scarlet blend and bloom in spring and fall. Slight fragrance; glossy foliage. Plants grow 8 to 15 feet tall. Introduced 1942.

CLIMBING MRS. SAM McGREDY. Climbing hybrid tea. Double blossoms, 3 to 5 inches across, are of a blend of scarlet, copper and orange and bloom in spring and fall. Moderate fragrance; glossy reddish bronze foliage. Plants grow 10 to 20 feet tall. Introduced 1937.

CLIMBING PEACE (also called Climbing Mme. A. Meilland). Climbing hybrid tea. Large double flowers, 4 to 5½ inches across, are golden yellow edged with pink and have a slight fragrance. Plants bloom abundantly in spring and fall after having been established for two or three years, and grow 15 to 20 feet tall. Introduced 1950.

CLIMBING PICTURE. Climbing hybrid tea. Velvety rose-pink double flowers, 2½ to 4½ inches across, have a slight fragrance and are surrounded by dark, glossy foliage. Plants bloom in spring and fall, growing 8 to 15 feet tall. Introduced 1942.

CLIMBING PINKIE. Climbing polyantha. Rose-pink semidouble flowers, 1½ to 2½ inches across, with 14 to 16 petals each, bloom in large clusters continuously throughout the season. Slight fragrance. Plants grow 8 to 12 feet tall. Introduced 1952.

CLIMBING QUEEN ELIZABETH. Climbing grandiflora. Double blossoms, 3 to 4 inches across, are rose and pale pink in color and bloom in spring and fall. Moderate fragrance; dark, glossy, leathery foliage. Plants grow 10 to 13 feet tall. Introduced 1957.

CLIMBING SHOT SILK. Climbing hybrid tea. Double blossoms, 3 to 4 inches across, are pink in color, shading to yellow at the base, and bloom on strong stems in spring and fall. Strong fragrance; glossy, slightly curled foliage. Plants grow 8 to 12 feet tall. Introduced 1931.

CLIMBING SHOW GARDEN (also called Pink Arctic). Large-flowered climber. Double blossoms, 4 to 5 inches across, are crimson that fades to rose and magenta. Moderate fragrance. Plants grow 6 to 12 feet tall and bloom in spring and fall. Introduced 1954.

COLONIAL WHITE. Large-flowered climber. White double blossoms, 2 to 3 inches across, are shaped like wide, flat cups and have a moderate fragrance. Plants grow 12 to 15 feet tall and bloom continuously. Introduced 1959.

CORAL DAWN. Large-flowered climber. Coral pink double blossoms, 4 to 5 inches across, bloom continuously. Moderate fragrance; leathery foliage. Plants grow 6 to 12 feet tall. Introduced 1952.

CORALITA. Large-flowered climber. Double blossoms, 3 to 4 inches across, are orange coral in color. Moderate fragrance; dark, leathery foliage. Plants grow 6 to 8 feet tall and bloom continuously. Introduced 1964.

DON JUAN

CORAL SATIN. Large-flowered climber. Coral-pink double blossoms, 3 to 4 inches across, bloom profusely and continuously. Moderate fragrance. Plants grow 6 to 8 feet tall and are exceptionally hardy. Introduced 1960.

DON JUAN. Large-flowered climber. Large double blossoms, up to 5 inches across, are velvety red and have a strong fragrance. Plants grow 6 to 10 feet tall, bloom continuously and make good pillar roses. Introduced 1958.

DORTMUND. Kordesii. Five- to 7-petaled single flowers, 2½ to 3½ inches across, are red with white centers and bloom in large clusters. Moderate fragrance. Plants grow 8 to 12 feet tall and bloom continuously. Introduced 1955.

DOUBLOONS. Large-flowered climber. Rich gold-yellow double blossoms, 3 to 4 inches across, are borne in clusters on strong stems. Moderate fragrance. Plants grow 10 to 15 feet tall and bloom in spring and fall. Introduced 1934.

DR. J. H. NICOLAS. Large-flowered climber. Rose-pink double blossoms, up to 5 inches across, are borne in clusters of 3 to 4 flowers. Moderate fragrance. Plants grow 7 to 8 feet tall and bloom continuously. Its stiff canes make this an excellent pillar rose. Introduced 1940.

DR. W. VAN FLEET. Large-flowered climber. Double blossoms 2½ to 3½ inches across are pink fading to flesh white and are borne on long, strong stems. Moderate fragrance; dark, glossy foliage. Plants grow 15 to 20 feet tall, bloom only in the spring. Introduced 1910.

ETERNAL FLAME. Large-flowered climber. Light orange semidouble flowers of 12 to 19 petals each are 3 to 4 inches in diameter and blossom in spring and fall. Moderate fragrance. Plants grow 10 to 15 feet tall. Introduced 1955.

GLADIATOR. Large-flowered climber. Double blossoms are 4 to 5 inches across and bright rose red in color. Moderate fragrance; dark, leathery foliage. Plants grow 10 to 12 feet high and bloom continuously. Introduced 1955.

GOLDEN SHOWERS. Large-flowered climber. Daffodil-yellow double blossoms, 3 to 4 inches across, have a moderate fragrance and bloom continuously. Plants are almost thornless, and grow 6 to 12 feet tall. Introduced 1956. All-America Rose Selection 1957.

MME. GRÉGOIRE STAECHELIN (also called Spanish Beauty). Large-flowered climber. Semidouble blossoms, 3 to 4 inches across, have less than 20 ruffled petals of delicate pink with crimson undersides, opening out to expose the center. Moderate fragrance; dark, glossy foliage, many thorns. Plants grow up to 14 feet tall and bloom once a year, in early spring. Introduced 1929.

MRS. ARTHUR CURTISS JAMES (also called Golden Climber). Large-flowered climber. Semidouble blossoms, 3½ to 5 inches across with 15 to 20 petals each, are a brilliant sunflower yellow; they bloom in the spring. Moderate fragrance; dark, glossy foliage. Plants grow up to 20 feet tall. Introduced 1933.

NEW DAWN (also called Everblooming Dr. W. Van Fleet). Large-flowered climber. Clusters of blush pink double blossoms, 2 to 3 inches across, are set in dark, glossy foliage. Slight fragrance. Plants grow 15 to 20 feet tall and bloom continuously. Introduced 1930.

DR. W. VAN FLEET

MME. GRÉGOIRE STAECHELIN

PARKDIREKTOR RIGGERS

PARKDIREKTOR RIGGERS. Kordesii. Velvety crimson semidouble flowers, 1½ to 2½ inches across with less than 20 petals each, are borne in large clusters of up to 50 blossoms. Slight fragrance. Plants grow about 12 feet tall and bloom continuously. Introduced 1957.

PAUL'S SCARLET CLIMBER. Large-flowered climber. Semidouble blossoms, 2 to 3 inches across with less than 20 petals each, are a vivid scarlet and bloom profusely in large clusters in the spring. Slight fragrance. Plants grow 10 to 15 feet tall. One of the most popular of all climbing roses. Introduced 1916.

PILLAR OF FIRE. Climbing floribunda. Double blossoms, 1½ to 2½ inches across, are coral red in color and have a slight fragrance. Plants grow 8 to 10 feet tall and bloom continuously. Introduced 1963.

PINK CAMEO (also called Climbing Cameo). Climbing miniature. Double blossoms, 1 to 1½ inches across, are rose pink with darker pink centers and grow in clusters of up to 20 flowers. Slight fragrance; rich, glossy foliage. Sometimes classified as a polyantha, Pink Cameo grows 3 to 5 feet tall and blooms continuously. Introduced 1954.

RED EMPRESS. Large-flowered climber. Deep red double blossoms, 3½ to 5 inches across, grow singly or two on a stem. Strong fragrance. Plants grow 8 to 12 feet tall and bloom continuously. Introduced 1956.

RHODE ISLAND RED. Large-flowered climber. Double blossoms, 4 to 5 inches across, are dark red and have a moderate fragrance. Plants grow 10 to 15 feet tall and bloom in spring and fall. Introduced 1957.

RHONDA. Large-flowered climber. Double blossoms, 3 to 4 inches across with about 40 petals each, are medium pink. Slight fragrance; glossy deep green foliage. Plants grow 7 to 8 feet tall and bloom profusely in the spring and continuously through summer. Introduced 1968.

RITTER VON BARMSTEDE. Kordesii. Semidouble blossoms, 1 to 2 inches across with about 20 petals each, are deep pink in color and are borne in large clusters of 30 to 40 flowers. No fragrance. Plants grow 10 to 12 feet tall and bloom continuously. Introduced 1959.

SPECTACULAR (also called Danse du Feu). Large-flowered climber. Scarlet double blossoms are 3 to 4 inches across and have a moderate fragrance. Glossy, bronze-green foliage. Plants grow 8 to 15 feet tall and bloom continuously. Introduced 1953.

VIKING QUEEN. Large-flowered climber. Double blossoms, 3 to 4 inches across with 60 petals each, are medium to deep pink and grow in large clusters. Strong fragrance; dark, glossy, leathery foliage. Plants grow 12 to 15 feet tall and bloom continuously. Introduced 1963.

WHITE DAWN. Large-flowered climber. Double blossoms, 2 to 3 inches across, are white and have a moderate fragrance. Plants grow 6 to 12 feet tall and bloom continuously. Introduced 1949.

ZEUS. Large-flowered climber. Double blossoms, 2 to 3 inches across, are golden yellow and have a slight fragrance. Dark, leathery foliage. Plants grow 15 to 20 feet tall and bloom continuously. Introduced 1959.

PINK CAMEO

ZWEIBRÜCKEN. Kordesii. Deep crimson double blossoms, 2 to 3 inches across, are borne in large clusters. Slight fragrance. Plants grow 6 to 10 feet tall and bloom continuously. Introduced 1955.

Polyantha roses

Polyantha roses are low, very hardy plants that continuously produce large clusters of small blooms and survive winters unprotected as far north as Zone 5 *(page 153)*. Indeed, "many blooms" is what the Greek word polyantha means. The blossoms are small, rarely exceeding 2 inches in diameter, and the plants are generally 2 feet or less in height, which makes them ideal for massing in beds and for use as low hedges. They are also widely grown by florists as house plants for Easter and Mother's Day, after which they may be set out in the garden. More than most roses, polyanthas bloom profusely not only on old canes but also on new canes that spring from or close to the ground. This tendency of polyanthas to have a number of canes and stems at different stages of maturity at the same time ensures a steady supply of flowers week after week.

Polyantha roses range in color from deep red all the way to white, with many lovely shades of pink; there are also some yellow, salmon and orange varieties. The blossoms are either doubles, with as many as 45 petals; semidoubles, with less than 20 petals; or singles, with five to seven petals. Only a very few varieties have much fragrance. But it is scent, as well as form and color, that helps account for the continued popularity, after almost a century, of the best known of the polyanthas, the bright pink-on-yellow, delicately fragrant Cécile Brunner, the original Sweetheart Rose. Other varieties have become less popular as polyanthas have to a great extent been replaced by their larger and more spectacular offspring, the floribundas, which were bred from polyanthas and hybrid teas.

CAROL ANN. Small double flowers, 1 to 1½ inches across, are orange salmon in color and bloom in tight clusters. No fragrance. Plants grow less than 2 feet tall. Introduced 1940.

CÉCILE BRUNNER (also called Mignon and Sweetheart Rose). Clusters of small, exquisite double flowers, 1 to 1½ inches across, bloom in bright pink with touches of yellow at the base of the petals. Moderate fragrance. Soft, dark, glossy foliage; very few thorns. This long-time favorite is one of the taller polyanthas, growing nearly 3 feet high. Introduced 1881.

DICK KOSTER FULGENS. Light red semidouble flowers are 1 to 1½ inches across and have fewer than 20 petals each. No fragrance. Plants grow less than 2 feet tall. Introduced 1940.

HAPPY. Named for one of the seven dwarfs in *Snow White,* this variety has large clusters of tiny semidouble flowers of less than 20 petals each, ½ to 1 inch across, currant red in color. No fragrance; dark, glossy foliage. Plants grow less than 2 feet tall. Introduced 1954.

CÉCILE BRUNNER

HAPPY

MARGO KOSTER

THE FAIRY

FRAU KARL DRUSCHKI

MARGO KOSTER (also called Sunbeam). Globular double flowers are 1 to 2 inches in diameter, and of a salmon color. Slight fragrance; few thorns. The plants, which grow less than 2 feet tall, are often sold in pots for indoor use and later planting outdoors. Introduced 1931.

MOTHERSDAY (also called Fête de Mères, Morsdag, and Muttertag). Clusters of up to 20 deep red double flowers, 1 to 2 inches across, bloom profusely on glossy-leaved plants less than 3 feet tall. No fragrance. As the name indicates, Mothersday is a popular gift in early May for indoor use and later planting. Introduced 1949.

ORANGE TRIUMPH. Semidouble flowers, 1 to 2 inches across with fewer than 20 petals each, are of a red and orange blend and bloom in large sprays. Slight fragrance. A relatively tall polyantha, growing up to 3 feet high, this rosebush is often used to form low hedges or to provide color accents in a garden. Introduced 1937.

SNOW WHITE. Globe-shaped white double flowers, 1 to 2 inches across, bloom in small clusters. No fragrance. Plants are bushy and grow less than 2 feet tall. Year of introduction unknown.

THE FAIRY. Large clusters of small, light pink double flowers, 1 to 1½ inches across, bloom profusely throughout the growing season. No fragrance; glossy foliage. Plants, which are especially hardy, grow 2 to 3 feet high and are often used in hedges. Introduced 1941.

Hybrid perpetual roses ·

Hybrid perpetuals are not much seen in rose catalogues today. Like the heavy furniture, beaded curtains and Tiffany lamps of the Victorian era, they are still around but their peak has passed. And what a peak it was; by the end of the 19th Century, some 3,000 varieties had been developed. The few that have proved timeless are valued for their hardiness, disease resistance and fragrance. They can be grown without winter protection in Zones 5-10 *(page 153)*.

Hybrid perpetuals are the first of the modern roses, concocted about 1840 from the damask, China and Bourbon dynasties. The second part of the name is misleading; when they were introduced, they did indeed blossom more steadily than any other class then available. But most varieties bloom profusely in June, then produce a more modest flowering in the fall, with occasionally, in some cases, a sprinkling of blossoms during the months in between.

The blossoms are large—up to 7 inches across—and most are fully doubled, with as many as 100 petals. A limited color range runs from white to deep maroon but includes no yellow. As compensation, Frau Karl Druschki, a lushly growing hybrid perpetual, is considered to be one of the finest of the white roses, and it is still widely grown.

The plants are rather tall, most varieties averaging 4 to 5 feet and some reaching twice that height. The leaves and thorns display the same wide range of shapes, colors and sizes as the hybrid teas. Best known of all the hybrid perpetuals is the famous American Beauty Rose. In the good old days, when a young man could still afford a dozen red roses, it was a dozen American Beauties that he held behind his back when he rang the doorbell of his best girl.

AMERICAN BEAUTY (also called Mme. Ferdinand Jamin). Large 3- to 4-inch double blossoms are a blend of light rose and dark pink. Strong fragrance; few thorns. Plants grow 4 to 5 feet tall and bloom continuously. Once the most popular rose sold by florists. Introduced 1886.

ARRILLAGA. Double blossoms, 3 to 5 inches across, are vivid pink with gold at the base of the petals. Moderate fragrance. Plants grow 5 to 8 feet tall on long, strong stems and bloom profusely in spring and fall. Introduced 1929.

BARON GIROD DE L'AIN. Medium-sized double flowers, 2 to 3 inches across, are red with white borders. Moderate fragrance; few thorns. Plants grow 3 to 5 feet tall and bloom in spring and fall. Introduced 1897.

BARONNE PRÉVOST. Rose-pink, flat double flowers are 3 to 4 inches across and have a moderate fragrance. Plants grow 4 to 5 feet tall and bloom in spring and fall. Introduced 1842.

BLACK PRINCE. Double blossoms, 3 to 4 inches across, are dark crimson with black at the base of the petals. Strong fragrance. Plants grow 3 to 5 feet tall and bloom in spring and fall. Introduced 1866.

CLIO. Satiny, flesh-pink double flowers, 3 to 4 inches across, are globular in shape and are borne in clusters on long, strong stems. Moderate fragrance. Plants grow 3 to 7 feet tall and bloom in spring and fall. Introduced 1894.

FERDINAND PICHARD. Double blossoms, 2½ to 4 inches across, are pink streaked with scarlet. No fragrance; light green foliage. Plants grow 4 to 6 feet tall and bloom in spring and fall. Introduced 1921.

FRAU KARL DRUSCHKI (also called Reine des Neiges, Snow Queen, White American Beauty). White double blossoms, sometimes with a blush-pink center, are 3 to 4 inches across and open out fully, exposing the centers. No fragrance. Plants grow 4 to 6 feet tall and bloom continuously. One of the finest white roses. Introduced 1901.

GÉANT DES BATAILLES (also called Giant of Battles). Fiery red double flowers, 3 to 4 inches across, have up to 85 petals each. Strong fragrance. Plants grow 3½ to 4 feet tall and bloom in spring and fall. Introduced 1846.

GÉNÉRAL JACQUEMINOT (also called General Jack, Jack Rose). Clear red double blossoms, 2½ to 4½ inches across, have soft, velvety petals and grow on long, strong stems. Strong fragrance; rich green foliage. Plants grow 4 to 6 feet tall and bloom in spring and fall. One of the earliest sold by florists and still popular. Introduced 1853.

GEORG ARENDS (also called Fortuné Besson). Large double blossoms, 3 to 5½ inches across, are of a soft pink color. Strong fragrance; few thorns. Plants grow 4 to 5 feet tall and bloom continuously. Introduced 1910.

HENRY NEVARD. Dark red double blossoms are 4 to 5 inches across and have a strong fragrance. Large, dark green, leathery leaves. An upright plant that grows 3 to 7 feet tall and blooms in spring and fall. Introduced 1924.

GÉNÉRAL JACQUEMINOT

GEORG ARENDS

HENRY NEVARD

127

MARCHIONESS OF LONDONDERRY PAUL NEYRON

HUGH DICKSON. Rich crimson double flowers, 2½ to 4 inches across, have a strong fragrance. Plants grow 8 to 10 feet tall and bloom in spring and fall. Introduced 1905.

JOHN HOPPER. Rose-pink double flowers with lilac edges and dark red centers are 3½ to 5 inches across and bear 70 petals each. Strong fragrance. A vigorous, upright, thorny plant that grows 4 to 5 feet tall and blooms in spring and sometimes in fall. Introduced 1862.

JULES MARGOTTIN. Large double flowers, 3 to 5 inches across, are shaped like wide, flat cups and have up to 90 petals each, of a medium pink color. Slight fragrance. An extremely hardy plant that grows 5 to 6 feet tall and blooms in spring and fall. Introduced 1853.

MABEL MORRISON. Large, high-centered double flowers, 4 to 5 inches across and shaped like cups, are flesh-colored, later fading to white. Moderate fragrance; grayish foliage. Plants grow 3 to 4 feet tall and bloom in spring and fall. Introduced 1878.

MARCHIONESS OF LONDONDERRY. Large 4- to 5-inch double flowers are white tinged with pale pink. Moderate fragrance. Sturdy, thornless plants grow 5 to 7 feet tall and bloom in spring and fall. Introduced 1893.

MRS. JOHN LAING. Double flowers, 3 to 4 inches across, are soft pink in color and have a strong fragrance. Few thorns. Plants grow 3 to 6 feet tall and bloom profusely and continuously. Introduced 1887.

PAUL NEYRON. Rose-pink double blossoms are shaped like wide, flat cups, 4 to 7 inches across. Moderate fragrance. Large, rich green leaves, few thorns. Plants grow 4 to 6 feet tall, are highly disease resistant and bloom in spring and fall. Introduced 1869.

PRINCE CAMILLE DE ROHAN (also called La Rosière). Velvety, dark red double blossoms, 3 to 4½ inches across, have up to 100 petals each and are borne on rather weak stems. Strong fragrance. Plants grow 3 to 6 feet tall, bloom in the spring and sometimes once more in the fall. Introduced 1861.

REINE DES VIOLETTES (also called Queen of the Violets). Flat double blossoms, 3½ to 4½ inches across, have up to 75 petals each of a mauve hue that fades to lavender. Strong fragrance. Smooth, glossy leaves; few thorns. Plants grow 5 to 8 feet tall, bloom profusely in spring and fall, bearing their flowers in clusters. Introduced 1860.

RUHM VON STEINFURTH (also called Red Druschki). Red double blossoms are 3 to 5 inches across and have a strong fragrance. Dark green, leathery foliage. Plants grow 4 to 5 feet tall and bloom profusely in spring and fall. Introduced 1920.

SOUVENIR DE MME. H. THURET. Large double flowers, 3 to 5 inches across, are salmon pink with yellow edges and red centers. Petals curve sharply under. Slight fragrance. Plants grow 3 to 5 feet tall and bloom continuously. Introduced 1922.

WALDFEE. Red double blossoms, 3 to 4 inches across, bloom in small clusters and have a moderate, spicy fragrance. Plants grow 5 to 10 feet tall and flower in spring and fall. Shiny, dark green foliage. Introduced 1960.

CATHERINE MERMET

Tea roses

Despite repeated crossbreedings, modern tea roses still resemble their Asiatic ancestors that arrived in Europe in the early 1800s. Their loosely formed blossoms, 2 to 3 inches across, have translucent petals of white, blush, clear pink, lemon yellow, sulfur, apricot, buff, fawn or salmon. The flowers are doubles, with as many as 50 petals; there are a few semidoubles with 10 to 20 petals. They have a delicate fragrance like that of fresh tea leaves, and appear alone or in clusters of two or three. The bushes spread wide and reach a height of 4 to 6 feet if not cut back by pruning or harmed by frost. Most varieties have finely serrated light green leaflets and straight red thorns.

Tea roses are thin stemmed and extremely susceptible to frost damage. They do not easily survive winters north of Zone 7, even with protection, but in Zones 8-10 they bloom vigorously and continuously from early February to late December. They are relatively resistant to black spot and powdery mildew.

CATHERINE MERMET. Double blossoms of flesh pink with lilac edges are 2 to 3 inches across. Moderate fragrance. Plants grow 3 to 4 feet tall. Introduced 1869.

DUCHESSE DE BRABANT. Rosy pink, tulip-shaped double blossoms are 2 to 3 inches across and have a strong fragrance. Plants grow 3 to 5 feet tall and are relatively disease resistant. The Duchesse de Brabant rose was a favorite of Theodore Roosevelt, who often wore one in his lapel while he was President. Introduced 1857.

MAMAN COCHET. Double blossoms, 3 to 4 inches across, are pale pink with yellow at the base of their petals. They have pointed buds and a moderate fragrance. Plants grow 3 to 4 feet tall. Introduced 1893.

MLLE. FRANZISKA KRÜGER. Double blossoms, 2 to 3 inches across, are coppery yellow and pink, sometimes with green centers. Moderate fragrance. Plants grow 3 to 4 feet tall. Relatively hardy for a tea rose. Introduced 1880.

MRS. DUDLEY CROSS. Pale yellow double blossoms, 2 to 3 inches across, are tinted crimson in the fall. Slight fragrance. Plants grow 2 to 4 feet tall. A thornless rose that lasts well after cutting. Introduced 1907.

SAFRANO. Apricot-colored semidouble blossoms, 2 to 3 inches across, have less than 20 petals each. Moderate fragrance. Plants grow to 4 feet tall. Introduced 1839.

SOMBREUIL. Double blossoms shaped like wide, flat cups, 2 to 4 inches across, have petals of creamy white, sometimes tinged with pink. Strong fragrance. A climbing tea that grows from 5 to 10 feet tall. Introduced 1850.

WHITE MAMAN COCHET. Two- to 3-inch double blossoms are white, sometimes tinged with pink. Moderate fragrance. Plants grow 2 to 5 feet tall. Introduced 1896.

WILLIAM R. SMITH. Double blossoms, 2 to 3 inches across, are of a pink-cream-yellow blend. Slight fragrance. Plants grow 3 to 5 feet tall and have long, strong stems with few thorns. Introduced 1908.

MAMAN COCHET

DUCHESSE DE BRABANT

SOMBREUIL

APOTHECARY ROSE

CARDINAL DE RICHELIEU

ROSA MUNDI

Old roses

The term "old roses" refers to a number of garden varieties that reached the limits of their development many years ago and have been largely superseded by newer types. Today they are grown for their historic significance (some were used for perfume and medicine as far back as the days of the Roman Empire), or as contrasts to newer roses, or to complement the period architecture of a home. But they are well worth growing for their own virtues. Most are hardy and require little maintenance, surviving even if neglected, and many grow in gracefully arching bushes that need little pruning. They are generally more fragrant than modern roses and many have striking and often heavy scents. Old roses are available from only a handful of nurseries and usually must be ordered by mail.

French roses

The oldest of this class are the French, or gallica, roses, which grow in bushes 2 to 6 feet high. The flowers come in all shades of red, from pale pink to purplish maroon, and even in red-and-white stripes. The blossoms may be five-petaled singles, or doubles with as many as 60 petals. Fragrance also varies, from strong and rich in some to none at all in others. The stems are almost thornless; the leaves are rough in texture and dark green; the buds are round and blunt; the hips, or seed pods, are large, red and round. Most French roses bloom only once, in spring or early summer. They are very hardy and will do well as far north as Zone 4 without winter protection *(page 153)*.

APOTHECARY ROSE (*Rosa gallica officinalis,* also called Double French Rose, Red Rose of Lancaster). Semidouble flowers, 2 to 3 inches across, are rose red and have a strong fragrance. Hips are large and deep red. Plants grow 3 to 5 feet tall. One of the first roses brought to America by the Pilgrims, who valued it for both beauty and medicinal purposes. Cultivated prior to 1500.

BELLE ISIS. Pale pink double flowers are 2 to 3 inches across and have a moderate fragrance. Plants grow as compact bushes 2½ to 4 feet tall. Introduced 1845.

CAMAIEUX. Semidouble flowers, 2½ to 3½ inches across with less than 20 petals each, are white with dramatic stripes of red that fade to purple and gray. Strong, spicy fragrance. Plants grow in erect bushes 2 to 4 feet tall. Introduced 1830.

CARDINAL DE RICHELIEU. Double flowers, 2 to 3 inches across, are a violet color that darkens to bluish purple with age. Slight fragrance. Plants grow as large bushes, 4 to 6 feet tall. One of the most popular French roses. Introduced 1840.

DÉSIRÉE PARMENTIER. Fully doubled flowers, 2 to 3 inches across, are a vivid pink. No fragrance. Compact bushes grow 4 to 6 feet tall. Date of introduction unknown.

DUC DE GUICHE. Double flowers, 3 to 4 inches across, are light violet red that turns to wine red. Slight fragrance. Plants grow 4 to 5 feet tall. Date of introduction unknown.

ROSA MUNDI (*Rosa gallica versicolor*). Two- to 3-inch semidouble flowers are striped red, pink and white with yellow stamens. Moderate fragrance. Plants grow 3½ to 5 feet tall. A chance mutation of *Rosa gallica officinalis*, Rosa Mundi is believed to have been named for Rosamonde, mistress of England's King Henry II. Cultivated prior to 1581.

TUSCANY. Velvety semidouble flowers, 2½ to 4 inches across, are deep crimson with conspicuous yellow stamens. Slight fragrance. Plants grow as vigorous, upright bushes 3 to 4 feet tall. Introduced 1596.

Damask roses

The damasks provide flowers in white and in shades of pink from pale to rose red. They grow in arching shrubs that can reach 8 feet, though most are from 3 to 5 feet high. Blossoms are semidouble or double with up to 60 petals and grow in long clusters, surrounded by foliage that is usually a downy gray; the scarlet hips are large and round. The canes are thorny and the pale green stems are weak. Aside from the Autumn Damask and varieties derived from it, which flower a second time in the fall, damasks bloom once each year, usually in June, sending forth the famous fragrance that has been used since the First Century B.C. in preparing attar of roses. The plants are disease resistant and hardy, and may be grown without winter protection in Zones 4-10 *(page 153)*.

CELSIANA. Loosely formed semidouble blossoms, 3 to 4 inches across, have crinkled, pale pink petals and bloom in clusters of three to five flowers. Moderate fragrance. Plants grow as compact, large-leaved bushes 3 to 5 feet tall. Cultivated prior to 1750.

CÉSONIE. Fully doubled flowers, 3 to 4 inches across, are dark pink and have no fragrance. Plants grow as compact bushes 4 to 5 feet tall. Date of introduction unknown.

DAMASK ROSE (*Rosa damascena*, also called Rose of Castile). Double flowers, 2½ to 3½ inches across, are red, pink or white, with occasional stripes. Strong fragrance. Plants grow 4 to 5 feet tall. An ancient rose from Asia Minor, and the original member of the damask family, it was introduced into Europe in the 16th Century.

GLOIRE DE GUILAN. Clear pink double flowers are 2½ to 4 inches across and have a strong fragrance. Plants grow as sprawling bushes 3 to 5 feet tall. Long used for the making of attar of roses in Iran, this variety was introduced to Europe and America in 1949.

LEDA (also called Painted Damask). Double flowers, 2½ to 4 inches across, are blush pink with crimson edges and sometimes bloom in the fall as well as the spring. Moderate fragrance. Attractive leaves are rounded and deep green. Plants grow as hardy bushes 3 to 5 feet tall. Introduced 1827.

MME. HARDY. Very full double flowers, 2½ to 3½ inches across, are white with occasional tints of light pink and bloom in clusters. Strong fragrance. Plants grow as thickly foliaged bushes 4 to 6 feet tall. Among the finest of white roses. Introduced 1832.

TUSCANY

CELSIANA

MME. HARDY

131

ROSE DES QUATRE SAISONS

ROSE DU ROI

YORK AND LANCASTER

OMAR KHAYYAM. Fully doubled flowers, 2 to 3 inches across, are light pink and have a moderate fragrance. Pale green, downy foliage contrasts with dark thorns. Plants grow as small bushes 2 to 3 feet tall. Reputedly the descendant of a plant grown on the grave of the Persian poet Omar Khayyam. Introduced 1893.

ROSE DES QUATRE SAISONS (*Rosa damascena semperflorens,* also called Four Seasons Rose, Autumn Damask). Double flowers, 3 to 4 inches across, have crumpled, deep pink petals and bloom almost continuously. Moderate fragrance; distinctive yellowish gray-green foliage. Plants grow vigorously, to a height of 3 to 4 feet. A variety of Autumn Damask was familiar to the ancient Romans as the Rose of Paestum. Date of introduction unknown.

ROSE DU ROI (also called Lee's Crimson Perpetual). Semidouble flowers, 2½ to 3½ inches across, are bright red with hints of violet and bloom in spring and fall. Strong fragrance. Plants grow 3 to 4 feet tall. A parent of many hybrid perpetual roses. Introduced 1815.

YORK AND LANCASTER (*Rosa damascena versicolor*). Semidouble flowers, 1½ to 2½ inches across with less than 20 petals each, are white, pink or a combination of the two and bloom in clusters of three to five on long stems. Moderate fragrance. Plants grow 4 to 7 feet tall. Named for the opposing sides in England's Wars of the Roses—York's symbol was a white rose, Lancaster's a red rose. Cultivated prior to 1700.

Moss roses

The moss roses, variants of cabbage roses *(page 134),* get their name from the tiny hairlike glands that cover their sepals and resemble moss. This growth is sticky to the touch and gives off a resinous odor much like that of balsam pine. Most varieties have large, globular flowers, with about 100 broad petals that curve in toward the center. The common colors are shades of pink, but some hybrid types are darker crimsons or purples. Most moss roses bloom only once, although 19th Century breeders created a number that bloom in spring and fall or almost continuously (these exceptions are noted below). The canes, which turn from red to green with age, are marked by long, strong thorns. Most moss roses grow to a moderate height, averaging about 5 feet, but some will reach 10 feet if supported. Like the majority of old roses, the mosses are quite hardy, and most may be grown as far north as Zone 4 without winter protection *(page 153).*

ALFRED DE DALMAS (also called Mousseline). High-centered double flowers, 2 to 3 inches across, are pale pink and bloom continuously. Moderate fragrance. Plants grow as compact bushes 2 to 4 feet tall and make excellent border hedges. Introduced 1855.

ANNI WELTER. Double flowers, 2 to 3 inches across, are dark pink and have a moderate fragrance. Plants grow 3 to 4 feet tall. Introduced 1906.

CAPITAINE JOHN INGRAM. Double, pomponlike flowers, 2 to 3 inches across, are reddish purple in color and have a moderate fragrance. Plants grow as dense bushes 3 to 5 feet tall with dark leaves and many fine thorns. Introduced 1854.

COMMUNIS (also called Common Moss, Old Pink Moss, Pink Moss). Well-formed double flowers, 2 to 3 inches across, are rosy pink. Moderate fragrance. Plants are exceptionally hardy and grow vigorously, 3 to 5 feet tall. One of the oldest and most popular of the moss roses. Introduced about 1696.

COMTESSE DE MURINAIS (also called White Moss). Double flowers, 2 to 3 inches across, turn white from flesh-pink buds. Moderate fragrance; blue-green foliage tinged with bronze. Plants are rather tender and grow as upright bushes 5 to 6 feet tall. Introduced 1843.

CRAMOISI FONCÉ VELOUTÉ. Double flowers, 2 to 3 inches across, are deep crimson and have a moderate fragrance. Plants grow 4 to 6 feet tall. A very old variety. Date of introduction unknown.

CRESTED MOSS (*Rosa centifolia cristata*, also called Chapeau de Napoléon, Crested Provence Rose). Well-shaped double flowers, 2 to 3 inches across, are pink and generally bloom in clusters. Moderate fragrance; heavy moss on the edges of the sepals. The plant, which is exceptionally hardy and disease resistant, grows 4 to 5 feet tall. A chance mutation of *Rosa centifolia*, Crested Moss was found growing on the wall of a ruined Swiss convent. Introduced 1827.

DEUIL DE PAUL FONTAINE. Semidouble flowers, 2 to 3½ inches in diameter with less than 20 petals each, are deep purplish red in color and bloom continuously, both singly and in clusters. They have no fragrance. The entire plant—flowers, foliage and canes—is unusually dark and grows as a very thorny bush 2 to 4 feet tall. Relatively tender. Introduced 1873.

GLOIRE DES MOUSSEUX. Large, symmetrical double flowers, 3 to 4 inches across, are salmon pink and bloom in clusters. Moderate fragrance. Plants grow as compact bushes 3 to 5 feet tall. Introduced 1852.

GOLDEN MOSS. Double flowers, 2 to 3½ inches across, are medium yellow and bloom in scanty clusters of 3 to 5 on long stems. Moderate fragrance; sepals are heavily mossed. Plants are very tender but vigorous and grow 6 to 8 feet tall. A relatively new variety for a moss rose. Introduced 1932.

HENRI MARTIN (also called Red Moss). Semidouble flowers, 2 to 3 inches across with less than 20 petals each, bloom crimson and then fade to a deep pink. No fragrance. Plants grow as loose, attractive bushes 4 to 6 feet tall. Introduced 1863.

JULIE DE MERSENT. Double flowers, 2 to 3 inches across, are blush pink and bloom profusely. Both flowers and foliage have moderate fragrance. Plants grow 4 to 5 feet tall. Date of introduction unknown.

LANEII (also called Lane's Moss). Double flowers, 2 to 3 inches across, are crimson with heavily mossed sepals. Moderate fragrance. Plants grow 4 to 5 feet tall. Introduced 1854.

LOUIS GIMARD. Cabbagelike buds open into full double flowers, 2 to 3½ inches across, that are bright pink and bloom on long stems. No fragrance. Plants grow 4 to 5 feet tall. Introduced 1877.

ALFRED DE DALMAS

CRESTED MOSS

GLOIRE DES MOUSSEUX

MME. LOUIS LÉVÊQUE   SALET

MME. LOUIS LÉVÊQUE. Lushly doubled flowers, 2½ to 3½ inches across, are bright salmon pink. They bloom in both spring and fall, and have a strong fragrance. Globular blossoms tend to close into a ball shape in damp weather. Plants grow as thorny bushes to a height of 4 to 6 feet. Introduced 1898.

NUITS DE YOUNG (also called Old Black). Small double flowers, 1½ to 2½ inches across, are dark reddish purple with yellow stamens and bloom in midsummer. No fragrance. Plants grow as wiry bushes with sparse foliage 3 to 5 feet tall. Introduced 1845.

SALET. Full double flowers, 2 to 3½ inches across, are rosy pink and open flat to reveal rows of small, closely packed petals. Strong musk fragrance. Plants are extremely hardy, grow as sturdy bushes 3 to 6 feet tall and bloom continuously. Introduced 1854.

VIOLACÉE. Double flowers, 2 to 3 inches across, are an unusual blend of purple, violet and pink. No fragrance. Plants grow 4 to 5 feet tall. Introduced 1876.

WHITE BATH (also called White Moss). Double flowers, 2 to 3 inches across, are white and have a strong fragrance. Plants grow 4 to 5 feet tall. A chance mutation of the pink Communis. Introduced 1810.

WILLIAM LOBB (also called Duchesse d'Istrie). Semidouble flowers, 2 to 3 inches across with less than 20 petals each, are crimson, fading to gray with age. They bloom in large clusters on strong stems and have no fragrance. Plants grow as tall, very thorny bushes 6 to 8 feet in height. Introduced 1855.

Cabbage roses

The cabbage roses are slender bushes with arching branches and drooping flowers and grow from 3 to 6 feet tall. Their red, pink or white flowers are 1 to 4 inches in diameter and have hollow centers. The flower petals often number up to 100, giving several varieties their name of *Centifolia;* their petals overlap in the manner of the leaves on a head of cabbage —hence the flower's more common species name. Cabbage roses are also sometimes called Provence roses, after the area in southeastern France where they were once widely grown. With few exceptions, cabbage roses have an exceedingly sweet fragrance. Their thorns are large and sometimes hooked, and their coarse foliage is wrinkled and serrated. Most varieties blossom only once a year, in late spring or early summer. Cabbage roses are extremely hardy and can be grown in Zones 4 to 10 without winter protection *(page 153)*.

ADELINE. Double flowers, 2 to 4 inches in diameter, come in a pink shade that grows paler toward the edges of the petals. The flowers have no fragrance. Plants grow as compact bushes 3 to 4 feet tall, with dark green foliage. Year of introduction unknown.

BLANCHEFLEUR. Double flowers, 2 to 3 inches across, are creamy white with blush pink centers. Moderate fragrance; red-tipped buds. Plants are vigorous and grow 3 to 5 feet tall. Introduced 1835.

PETITE DE HOLLANDE

FANTIN-LATOUR. Flat double flowers, 2 to 3 inches in diameter, are light pink and bloom singly or in pairs. They have a moderate fragrance and dark green leaves. Plants grow as rounded bushes 4 to 6 feet tall. Year of introduction unknown.

PARKJUWEL (also called Park Jewel). Well-formed, fully doubled flowers, 2 to 4 inches across, are light pink and bloom profusely in clusters. They have a strong fragrance and light green, wrinkled foliage. Plants grow as attractive bushes with arching branches, 3 to 4 feet tall, but are not as hardy as other cabbage roses. Parkjuwel was bred from a moss rose and is sometimes listed under that category. Introduced 1956.

PETITE DE HOLLANDE (also called Petite Junon de Hollande). Small pink double flowers, 1½ to 2½ inches across, are exquisitely formed and grow in clusters. Moderate fragrance. Plants, which average 3 to 4 feet in height, have long been popular for smaller gardens. Year of introduction unknown.

PROLIFERA DE REDOUTÉ. Double flowers, 2 to 3 inches in diameter, are pink and extremely full, often with another bud growing from the center. Moderate fragrance. This variety resembles the original cabbage rose except for its sepals, which are longer and more fringed. Plants grow 4 to 6 feet tall and have weak stems and canes. Date of introduction unknown.

RED PROVENCE. Cupped double flowers, 2 to 3 inches across, are dark red and have a strong fragrance. Plants grow as low, spreading bushes 3 to 4 feet tall and are quite hardy. Year of introduction unknown.

ROSA CENTIFOLIA (also called Cabbage or Provence Rose). Lushly doubled pink flowers, 2 to 3 inches across with up to 100 overlapping petals each, grow singly on long slender stems. Moderate fragrance. Plants grow 5 to 6 feet tall, are extremely hardy, and have rounded, drooping leaves. Cultivated 1596.

ROSA CENTIFOLIA BULLATA. Large double blossoms, 3½ to 4½ inches across, are deep pink in color and have a strong fragrance. Handsome foliage resembling lettuce leaves hangs loosely from the stalks. The leaves change from green through bronze to red and brownish purple as the plant matures. Plants are very hardy and grow 4 to 6 feet tall. Originated before 1815.

ROSE DE MEAUX. Small double flowers, 1 to 1½ inches across, are light pink in color and have a strong fragrance. Bushes are small, growing 1½ to 3 feet in height, with pale green leaves. Introduced 1789.

ROSE DES PEINTRES (also called Painter's Rose). Double flowers, 2 to 3 inches across, are light pink in color, with a moderate fragrance. A very hardy and vigorous bush growing 5 to 6 feet tall, the Rose des Peintres is so named because it was often portrayed in 18th Century Dutch paintings. Year of introduction unknown.

VIERGE DE CLÉRY (also called Unique Blanche). Red buds open into white double blossoms that are sometimes tinged with pink and measure 2 to 3 inches across. Moderate fragrance. Plants are extremely hardy, bloom in late summer, after most other cabbage roses, and grow 4 to 5 feet tall. Introduced 1888.

ROSA CENTIFOLIA BULLATA

ROSE DE MEAUX

ROSE DES PEINTRES

BELINDA

BUFF BEAUTY

ERFURT

Hybrid musk roses

Exceptionally vigorous plants that provide almost continuous blooms, hybrid musks fall between bush roses and climbers in structure and habit of growth. The sturdy canes of these semiclimbers qualify them as good pillar roses—some types will grow to a height of 10 feet. Their glossy foliage is disease and pest resistant. Blooming in clusters of blossoms that range from simple five-petaled flowers to ones of 40 petals, most hybrid musks have a distinctive fruity fragrance. Most come in soft pastel colors, with reddish foliage and pink-to-orange-to-red hips that persist into very cold weather. Hybrid musks are generally less hardy than other old roses; they can be grown as far north as Zone 5 but need winter protection there.

BELINDA. Tiny semidouble flowers, 1 inch or less across, with less than 20 petals each, bloom almost continuously in soft pink clusters. Moderate fragrance. Plants grow as erect bushes 4 to 8 feet tall, are exceptionally hardy and make good hedges or pillar roses. Introduced 1936.

BISHOP DARLINGTON. Semidouble flowers, 2 to 3 inches across, with 16 to 18 petals each, range from cream to flesh pink, with yellow shadings. Moderate fruity fragrance; orange-scarlet buds. Plants are sturdy and grow 4 to 10 feet tall; larger ones are used as climbers. Introduced 1928.

BLOOMFIELD DAINTY. Single flowers of five to seven petals each are 2 to 3 inches across and bloom in bright yellow clusters. Moderate fragrance; orange buds. Plants grow 4 to 6 feet tall. Introduced 1924.

BUFF BEAUTY. Double flowers, 2 to 3 inches across, are of an orange-yellow blend. Moderate fragrance. Plants grow as graceful spreading bushes 4 to 6 feet tall and equally wide. Introduced 1939.

ERFURT. Semidouble flowers, 2 to 3 inches across with less than 20 petals each, are deep pink with yellow centers and have a strong musk fragrance. Foliage is wrinkled and leathery. Plants grow vigorously as drooping bushes 5 to 6 feet tall. Introduced 1939.

GRANDMASTER. Semidouble flowers of 10 petals each are 3 to 4 inches across, and are apricot yellow with a hint of pink. Moderate fragrance; light green foliage. Plants grow 3 to 6 feet tall. Introduced 1954.

KATHLEEN. Single flowers of five to seven petals each are 1 to 1½ inches across and blossom in large, long-stemmed clusters of blush pink. Slight fragrance; hips turn orange in the fall. Plants are hardy and vigorous, growing 6 to 15 feet tall, and can be trimmed as shrubs or trained as climbers. Introduced 1922.

PROSPERITY. Double flowers, 2½ to 3½ inches across, blossom white with pale yellow centers from creamy pink buds. The pattern of large flower clusters resembles that of a giant polyantha. Strong fragrance. Plants grow as high bushes, 6 to 12 feet tall. Introduced 1919.

ROSALEEN. Double flowers, 3 to 4 inches across, are dark red in color and blossom in large clusters. No fragrance. Plants grow 4 to 5 feet tall and are exceptionally hardy. Introduced 1933.

WILL SCARLET. Semidouble flowers, 2 to 3 inches across with less than 20 petals each, are scarlet and bloom continuously. Big clusters of orange hips appear in the fall. Moderate fragrance. Plants grow vigorously 5 to 8 feet tall, and do as well in partial shade as they do in full sunshine. Introduced 1956.

Alba roses

Albas are often associated with the White Rose of York, made famous in England's Wars of the Roses. The *Rosa alba (below)*, cultivated in Europe since 100 A.D. or before, may well have been York's emblem although the earliest record of albas actually growing in England is from 1597, 112 years after the wars ended. These roses resist disease and are extremely hardy, thriving as far north as Zone 4 without winter protection *(page 153)*. They grow on dense bushes 5 to 8 feet tall, in delicate shades of pink or white. The flowers are medium sized and range from five to 45 petals, depending on the variety; they are borne in clusters on stout, green, thorny canes with dusty, gray-green foliage. Albas bloom once, for about a month, in late spring or early summer. Most types have a hyacinth-like fragrance. Their hips are large, long and scarlet.

BELLE AMOUR. Semidouble flowers, 3 to 4 inches across, with less than 20 petals each, are soft pink with prominent yellow stamens. Moderate fragrance. Plants grow 5 to 6 feet tall. A very old variety, believed to be a cross of alba and damask roses. Date of introduction unknown.

CHLORIS. Double flowers, 3 to 4 inches across, are a rich blush pink with deeper pink centers. Moderate fragrance; dark, leathery leaves; few thorns. Plants grow as sturdy bushes 4 to 5 feet tall. Date of introduction unknown.

GREAT MAIDEN'S BLUSH *(Rosa alba incarnata)*. Double flowers, 2 to 3 inches across, are warm blush pink, fading with age to pale pink. Moderate fragrance. Plants grow as large bushes 4 to 8 feet tall with attractive arching branches and clustered blooms. Cultivated prior to 1738.

JEANNE D'ARC. Double flowers, 2 to 3 inches across, blossom creamy pink and fade to ivory white. No fragrance. Dense bushes grow 4 to 5 feet tall. Introduced 1818.

KÖNIGIN VON DÄNEMARK. Well-formed double flowers, 2½ to 4 inches across, are flesh pink with deep pink centers and have a strong fragrance. Foliage is an attractive dark blue-green. Plants grow as loose, spreading bushes 4 to 6 feet tall. Introduced 1826.

MME. LEGRAS DE ST. GERMAIN. Double flowers, 3 to 4 inches across, are white with pale yellow centers, unusual for albas. Moderate fragrance. Plants grow as slender, thornless bushes 6 to 7 feet tall. Introduced 1846.

ROSA ALBA (White Rose of York, also called Bonnie Prince Charlie's Rose, Jacobite Rose). The original version has single, five-petaled white flowers, but hybridized semidouble and double varieties, 2 to 3 inches across, have as many as 45 petals. All versions bloom profusely. Moderate fragrance. Hips turn scarlet in the fall. Plants grow 6 to 8 feet tall. Cultivated prior to 100 A.D.

WILL SCARLET

KÖNIGIN VON DÄNEMARK

GREAT MAIDEN'S BLUSH

HERMOSA

MARÉCHAL NIEL

MME. ERNST CALVAT

Bourbon, Noisette and China roses

The three classes of roses known as Bourbon, Noisette and China (the last sometimes called Bengal because it was first shipped to Europe from Bengal in the late 18th Century) are descended from common ancestors that grew in the subtropics of China and thus share several traits: They are not very hardy, especially the Noisettes, which should be grown only in the mild climates of Zones 8-10 without winter protection *(page 153)*. Almost all flower repeatedly; all have thick leaves, smooth hips and large, often curved thorns; and all usually bear their blossoms in clusters. Bourbons and Chinas come in white, pink, red and purple (some Bourbon varieties are striped); Noisettes come in all of these colors plus yellow.

In other ways the classes are dissimilar. Bourbons grow in compact shrubs usually 5 to 6 feet high, although some can reach a height of 12 feet. Noisettes are climbers that generally reach heights of 10 to 15 feet but may become straggly if unsupported. The Chinas range from low-growing varieties, ideal for borders because they rarely exceed 3 feet in height, to 6-foot-tall hybrids. Most Chinas have a bananalike fragrance, but Bourbons have an apple scent, and Noisettes give off the odor of tea roses, from which they are descended. The color of Bourbon foliage ranges from light to dark green and is often tinted with copper, red or purple when the plant is young; its texture is frequently leathery. China roses may also have red-tinged stems, but their foliage is glossy. Noisettes have smooth, oval leaves of light to medium green. The number of petals, depending on variety, ranges from five to 50 in Bourbons and Chinas and five to 80 in Noisettes.

COMMANDANT BEAUREPAIRE. Bourbon rose. Round, cupped double flowers, 2 to 3 inches across, are pink streaked with purple and white. Moderate fragrance. Plants grow 4 to 7 feet tall. Introduced 1874.

GREEN ROSE (*Rosa chinensis viridiflora*). China rose. An oddity of the rose world, this variety has green petals that are actually multiple sepals. The flowers are small, about 1 to 1½ inches across, and have no fragrance. Plants grow 3 to 5 feet tall. Introduced 1855.

HERMOSA. China rose. Pink double flowers, 1 to 3 inches across, bloom abundantly in clusters. Moderate fragrance; bluish green foliage. Plants grow 2 to 2½ feet tall and are tender. Introduced 1840.

MARÉCHAL NIEL. Noisette. Large double flowers, 2 to 3½ inches across, are golden yellow in color and bloom profusely. Strong fragrance; lush green foliage on delicate stems. Plants grow to a height of 8 to 15 feet when supported as climbers. Not hardy in northern climates. Introduced 1864.

MME. ERNST CALVAT. Bourbon rose. Double flowers, 2 to 3 inches across, come in shades of pink. Moderate fragrance. Foliage is wine red when new and darkens with age. Plants grow 6 to 8 feet tall and make good pillar roses. Introduced 1888.

MME. PIERRE OGER. Bourbon rose. Double flowers, 1½ to 2½ inches across, are of a rose-tinged lilac hue.

Strong fragrance. Plants grow 5 to 6 feet tall and bloom profusely and continuously. Introduced 1878.

OLD BLUSH (also called Common Monthly, Old Pink Daily, Old Pink Monthly, Parson's Pink China). China rose. Pink semidouble blooms, 1½ to 2½ inches across with less than 20 petals each, grow in clusters of about 15 flowers. Slight fragrance. Plants grow 3 to 5 feet tall, are tender and bloom continuously. Introduced 1752.

REINE VICTORIA (also called La Reine Victoria). Bourbon rose. Cupped double flowers, 1½ to 2½ inches across, are pink and grow in clusters. Moderate fragrance; soft green foliage. Plants grow to a height of 5 to 6 feet and bloom continuously. Introduced 1872.

SOUVENIR DE LA MALMAISON (also called Queen of Beauty and Fragrance). Bourbon rose. Double flowers, 1½ to 3½ inches across, are pink and have a strong, spicy fragrance. Plants grow 2 to 3 feet high, are tender and bloom continuously. Introduced 1843.

VARIEGATA DI BOLOGNA. Bourbon rose. Double blossoms, 3 to 4 inches across, are white with streaks of magenta and grow in clusters of three to five flowers. Strong fragrance. Plants grow from 6 to 10 feet tall, have strong canes with neat, narrow leaves and are used as shrubs or pillar roses. Introduced 1909.

ZÉPHIRINE DROUHIN. Bourbon rose. Open semidouble flowers, 2 to 4 inches across with less than 20 petals each, are pink in color with white at their bases. Moderate fragrance; tender; no thorns. Copper-purple leaves turn a rich green as the plant matures. Plants grow 5 to 15 feet tall. Introduced 1868.

Sweetbrier (eglantine) roses

Sweetbrier roses, also known as eglantine roses, derive their common name from their sweet fragrance and thick, thorny habit of growth. Their gracefully arched branches grow 8 to 12 feet tall. Their blossoms, five petaled except in a few hybrids, are bright pink, red, copper or yellow, and appear singly or in clusters. The flowers are about 1½ inches in diameter and are surrounded by roundish leaves approximately 1½ inches long that are dark green on the upper surface and grayish on the underside; the leaves give off an apple fragrance that is especially strong on humid days. Most sweetbriers bloom once each year, in late spring or early summer, but the leaves retain their fragrance throughout the growing season. Many types of sweetbrier roses produce an enormous number of hips, small and either round or oval in shape, depending on the variety; their orange-red hue lends color to gardens well into autumn and even winter. Sweetbrier stems are abundantly thorny, and if left untended the bushes become impenetrable thickets. But because of their compact growth habit, they can be trained into excellent hedges. Vigorous growers, sweetbriers are hardy enough to survive in Zones 4 to 10 without winter protection *(page 153)*.

AMY ROBSART. Semidouble flowers, 1 to 3 inches across with under 20 petals each, are rose pink in color. Both flow-

MME. PIERRE OGER   REINE VICTORIA

ZÉPHIRINE DROUHIN

139

LORD PENZANCE

ROSA EGLANTERIA

SUTTER'S GOLD (HYBRID TEA)

ers and leaves are fragrant. Plants grow 6 to 10 feet tall and bloom freely. Introduced 1894.

FLORA McIVOR. Clusters of small single flowers, 1 to 2 inches across with five to seven petals each, are white with pink shadings. Both flowers and leaves have a strong fragrance. Plants grow 6 to 12 feet tall. Introduced 1894.

LADY PENZANCE (*Rosa penzanceana*). Single flowers, 1 to 3 inches across with five to seven petals each, are an unusual coppery pink in color with yellow stamens. The leaves are more fragrant than the flowers. Plants are vigorous and grow 4 to 10 feet tall. Introduced 1894.

LORD PENZANCE. Yellow single flowers, 1½ to 3 inches across with five to seven petals each, grow in small clusters. Both flowers and leaves are fragrant. Plants are strong stemmed, grow 4 to 10 feet tall and bloom profusely. Named after a famed English jurist who was also an accomplished rose grower. Introduced 1894.

ROSA EGLANTERIA (also called Eglantine, Sweetbrier Rose). Small pink single flowers, 1 to 2 inches across with five to seven petals each, appear singly or in small clusters. Apple-scented foliage; oval hips. Plants grow 6 to 10 feet tall and are used to form attractive hedges. The "fragrant Eglantine" mentioned by Shakespeare, and the first of the sweetbriers, *Rosa eglanteria* is credited with unusual longevity, specimens having been found still growing in the long-deserted gardens of ruined castles. Cultivated prior to 1551.

Special purpose roses

Some roses are grown for particular effects in the garden and for this reason are often grouped in what are called special-purpose classes:

Tree roses

These roses, which look like small trees, are man-made plants that may be of almost any rose variety. They usually consist of three plants: a sturdy rootstock onto which is budded another rose variety that produces a sturdy trunk, or standard, which in turn supports a budded-on plant that forms the flower-bearing crown. Nurseries sometimes combine the first two steps by growing a strong rootstock that also produces a tall standard, but in either case the process is slow and takes skill; for this reason a rose variety costs several times more in tree form than it does as a bush.

Because the tender bud joint at the top of the standard is very vulnerable to frost damage, most tree roses are hardy enough to survive winter weather without protection only in Zones 8-10 *(page 153);* elsewhere, gardeners must wrap them snugly, or partially dig them up and bury them flat in the ground, unearthing and erecting them when spring comes *(page 63).*

Varieties with strong, upright stems like hybrid teas are the most popular tree roses; their round, stately crowns of blossoms make a striking sight, especially in formal gardens. Climbers also create spectacular effects: when weighted with flowers, their long, pliant stems droop over like graceful weeping willows.

Shrub roses

Toughness characterizes the group known as shrub roses, which are hardy enough to survive winters without protection even in Zone 4. Many are so-called species roses—their genetic characteristics are so firmly established that their seeds produce nearly uniform progeny, and they can be considered distinct botanical species. A number are so tough they will grow in the wild and in poor soil. Large and luxuriant plants, they can be grown singly, but are often planted in groups to provide a bold effect of massed color in hedges and screen plantings. Shrub roses vary considerably in height, growing from 2 to 10 feet tall; the average is between 6 and 8 feet. Their blossoms come in white and shades of pink, red, yellow, orange and purple. Most of the older varieties bloom only once, during the spring, but the newer types bloom almost continuously from spring until frost. Many varieties also produce colorful red hips that are decorative in autumn gardens. Some bear the wild roses' five-petaled single blossoms but others have many-petaled flowers; their fragrance also varies, from none to strong.

AGNES. Pale amber double blossoms are 2 to 3 inches across and have a moderate fragrance. Plants grow 4 to 6 feet tall and bloom profusely once in spring or early summer. Introduced 1922.

BLANC DOUBLE DE COUBERT. White double blossoms are 2 to 3 inches across. Strong fragrance. Plants grow 3 to 7 feet tall and bloom in spring and fall. Introduced 1892.

FRAU DAGMAR HARTOPP (also called Fru Dagmar Hastrup). Abundant silvery pink single blossoms are 2 to 3 inches in diameter and have five to seven petals each. Strong fragrance. Plants grow 2½ to 5 feet tall and bloom continuously. Introduced 1914.

FRÜHLINGSGOLD (also called Spring Gold). Red buds open into golden yellow single blossoms, 2 to 3 inches across with five to seven petals each. Strong fragrance; sturdy stems. Plants grow 6 to 10 feet tall and bloom profusely in spring or early summer. Introduced 1951.

FRÜHLINGSMORGEN. Single blossoms, 3 to 4 inches across with five to seven petals each, are cherry pink with yellow centers and maroon stamens. Moderate fragrance; large red hips. Plants grow 5 to 7 feet tall and bloom in spring and sometimes in fall. Introduced 1942.

GOLDEN WINGS. Large sulfur-yellow single blossoms, 4 to 5 inches across, have five to seven petals each. Slight fragrance. Hardy and vigorous plants grow 4 to 8 feet tall and bloom profusely in spring and fall. Introduced 1956.

GROOTENDORST SUPREME. Tiny double blossoms, ¾ to 1 inch across, are deep red in color and have serrated petals that make the flowers resemble carnations. No fragrance. Plants grow 4 to 7 feet tall and bloom in spring and fall. Introduced 1936.

HANSA. Double blossoms, 3 to 4 inches across, are reddish violet in color. Strong clove fragrance; short, weak stems and large red hips. Plants grow 4 to 5 feet tall and bloom in spring and fall. Introduced 1905.

BLANC DOUBLE DE COUBERT

FRAU DAGMAR HARTOPP

FRÜHLINGSGOLD

HARISON'S YELLOW. Small, open semidouble blossoms, 1½ to 2 inches across, have 10 to 14 petals each, bright yellow in color. Strong fragrance; rich green foliage; brownish black hips. Plants grow 5 to 8 feet tall and bloom profusely in spring or early summer. Introduced 1830.

MABELLE STEARNS. Lushly doubled blossoms, 2 to 3 inches across with 50 to 60 petals each, are peach pink and bloom in clusters. Strong fragrance. Plants grow only 1 to 2 feet tall but spread 6 to 8 feet wide; they bloom continuously. Introduced 1938.

MAX GRAF. Single blossoms, 2 to 3 inches across with five to seven petals each, are bright pink with golden centers and have a slight fragrance. An exceptionally hardy, trailing plant that seldom reaches 2 feet in height and makes an excellent ground cover. Blooms once in spring or early summer. Introduced 1919.

NEVADA. Pink buds open into large white single blossoms, 4 to 5 inches across with five to eight petals each; undersides are sometimes splashed with red. No fragrance. Light green foliage on short, nearly thornless stems. A profusely flowering shrub that grows 5 to 8 feet tall and blooms in spring and fall. Introduced 1927.

PINK GROOTENDORST. Tiny, pink double blossoms, ¾ to 1 inch across, have serrated petals and no fragrance. Plants grow 3½ to 4 feet tall and bloom in spring and fall. Introduced 1923.

POULSEN'S PARK ROSE. Large, silvery pink double blossoms, 4 to 5 inches across, have high centers that make them resemble hybrid tea roses. No fragrance; shiny foliage. A wide-spreading bush that grows 2½ to 6 feet tall and blooms continuously. Introduced 1953.

PRAIRIE DAWN. Pink double blossoms are about 2 inches across and have no fragrance. Plants grow 5 to 6 feet tall and bloom in spring and fall. A very hardy, upright plant whose name derives from the fact that it thrives even on prairies. Introduced 1959.

PRAIRIE FIRE. Double blossoms, 2 to 3 inches across, are bright red with white bases and are borne in clusters of 35 to 50 flowers. Moderate fragrance; glossy dark foliage. Plants are very hardy, grow 5 to 6 feet tall and bloom profusely in spring and fall. Introduced 1960.

ROBIN HOOD. Clusters of cherry red semidouble blossoms are 1 to 2 inches across, with less than 20 petals each. No fragrance. A compact bushy plant suitable for hedges, Robin Hood grows 4 to 5 feet tall and blooms in spring and fall. Introduced 1927.

ROSA FOETIDA BICOLOR (also called Austrian Copper). Single blossoms, 2 to 3 inches across with five to seven petals each, are orange scarlet with yellow undersides. Some rose growers find the scent unpleasant. Plants are very hardy, grow 4 to 6 feet tall and bloom once, in spring or early summer. Introduced before 1590.

ROSA FOETIDA PERSIANA (also called Persian Yellow). Bright yellow double blossoms, 2 to 3½ inches across, are borne directly on the canes. No fragrance; small leaves. A hardy and ancient plant from Persia that grows 4 to 5 feet tall and blooms once, in spring or early summer. Introduced 1837.

HARISON'S YELLOW

ROSA FOETIDA BICOLOR   MABELLE STEARNS

ROSA HUGONIS (also called Father Hugo Rose, Golden Rose of China). Light yellow single blossoms, about 2 inches in diameter with five to seven petals each, are borne on gracefully drooping branches. No fragrance. Plants grow 6 to 8 feet tall and bloom once a year, in spring or early summer. Introduced 1899.

ROSA MOYESII. Five-petaled single blossoms, 1½ to 2½ inches across, are of a deep red and pink blend. No fragrance; large, handsome orange-red hips. Plants grow up to 10 feet tall and bloom once a year, in spring or early summer. Introduced 1894.

ROSA RUBRIFOLIA. Tiny pink single flowers, about an inch in diameter, have five to seven petals each. No fragrance; reddish foliage; scarlet hips. Plants grow 6 to 8 feet tall and bloom once a year, in spring or early summer. Introduced 1830.

ROSA RUGOSA (also called Japanese Rose). Single, purplish red blossoms are 2½ to 3½ inches across with five to seven petals each. Moderate fragrance; shiny, dark green wrinkled foliage. A very hardy plant that grows 5 to 6 feet tall and blooms in spring and fall. Introduced 1845.

ROSA RUGOSA ALBA (also called White Japanese Rose). Single white blossoms are 2 to 3 inches across, with five to seven petals each. Moderate fragrance; orange-red hips. A very bushy plant that grows 5 to 7 feet tall and blooms in spring and fall. Introduced 1845.

ROSE À PARFUM DE L'HAY (also called Parfum de l'Hay). Cherry red double blossoms are 3 to 4 inches across and have a pungent, clovelike fragrance. Plants are tender, grow 4 to 6 feet tall and bloom profusely in spring and fall. Introduced 1901.

SARAH VAN FLEET. Clusters of medium pink semidouble blossoms, 4 to 5 inches across, have fewer than 20 petals each. Strong fragrance; dark, leathery foliage. Plants grow 6 to 10 feet tall and bloom abundantly and continuously. Introduced 1926.

SCHNEEZWERG (also called Snowdwarf). Semidouble blossoms, 1 to 2 inches across with less than 20 petals each, are white with yellow stamens and grow in clusters of three to 10 flowers. No fragrance; glossy foliage. Plants grow 3 to 4 feet tall and bloom in spring and fall. Abundant red hips appear concurrently with the fall blooming. Introduced 1912.

SPARRIESHOOP. Light pink single blossoms are 3 to 4 inches across with five to seven petals each. Strong fragrance; foliage is leathery and copper colored when young. Plants grow 4 to 12 feet tall and bloom in spring and fall. Introduced 1953.

STADT ROSENHEIM. Orange-red double blossoms, 2 to 3 inches across, grow in clusters of up to 10 flowers. Moderate fragrance; glossy, light green leaves. Plants grow 4 to 5 feet tall and bloom profusely once a year, in spring or early summer. Introduced 1961.

THÉRÈSE BUGNET. Double blossoms, 3 to 4 inches across, are of a red that fades to pink as the flower ages. Moderate fragrance. A very hardy plant that grows 4 to 6 feet tall and blooms once a year, in spring or early summer. Introduced 1950.

ROSA HUGONIS   SARAH VAN FLEET

SPARRIESHOOP

BABY GOLD STAR

BO-PEEP

DWARFKING

Miniature roses

At the opposite end of the scale from the tall shrub roses are the low-growing miniature roses, which are especially popular as edgings for beds and borders, as accent plants in small rock gardens and as house plants. There are more than 200 varieties of miniatures, ranging in height from 4 to 18 inches, with the average about 1 foot. Exceptions are a few miniature climbing roses that sprawl along the ground, if not supported, to a distance of 5 feet. It is even possible to buy miniature tree roses that stand 10 to 14 inches high. Most miniatures bloom continuously from spring to frost, producing clusters of ½- to 2-inch blossoms in a complete range of rose colors—white through pink, red, yellow, orange and purple—with petals that number five through 70, depending on the variety. In full bloom the flowers of most varieties open widely; most have little or no fragrance.

Despite their small size and delicate appearance, miniatures are hardy enough to survive winters in Zones 6-10 without protection.

BABY BETSY McCALL. Light pink double flowers, ¾ to 1 inch across, bloom profusely on compact bushes 8 to 10 inches tall. Moderate fragrance. Introduced 1960.

BABY DARLING. Double flowers, 1 to 1½ inches across, are of an orange-pink blend. No fragrance. Plants grow 12 to 14 inches tall and are relatively tender. Introduced 1964.

BABY GOLD STAR (also called Estrellita de Oro). Golden yellow semidouble to double flowers, 1½ to 2 inches in diameter, have 10 to 30 petals each. Slight fragrance. A larger-than-average miniature, growing 16 to 18 inches tall. Introduced 1940.

BABY MASQUERADE (also called Baby Carnaval). Double flowers, ¾ to 1 inch across, are of a red-yellow blend and bloom profusely. Slight, fruity fragrance. Plants grow 6 to 8 inches tall and are exceptionally hardy and disease resistant. Introduced 1956.

BEAUTY SECRET. High-centered double flowers, resembling those of hybrid teas, are 1 to 1½ inches across and colored a bright cardinal red. Strong fragrance. Plants grow 8 to 10 inches tall and are very hardy. Introduced 1965.

BO-PEEP. Tiny double blossoms are less than an inch across and rosy pink in color. Slight fragrance. Among the smallest of the miniatures, Bo-Peep grows 5 to 8 inches tall and is regarded as one of the finest of its type, though relatively tender. Introduced 1950.

CHIPPER. Salmon pink, high-centered double flowers, ½ to 1 inch across, bloom profusely on plants 15 to 18 inches tall. Slight fragrance. Relatively tender. Introduced 1966.

CINDERELLA. Double flowers, ¾ to 1 inch across, have 45 to 60 petals each, white with pink edges. Moderate, spicy fragrance. The plant grows as a thornless, upright bush, 12 to 15 inches tall, and is one of the most popular miniatures. Introduced 1953.

DWARFKING (also called Zwergkönig). Medium red double flowers, ¾ to 1 inch across, blossom both singly and in clusters. Slight fragrance. Plants grow 8 to 10 inches tall and are hardy and disease resistant. Introduced 1957.

OAKINGTON RUBY. Double flowers, 1 to 1½ inches across, are ruby crimson with white centers. No fragrance. Plants grow 10 to 12 inches tall. Introduced 1933.

OPAL JEWEL. Double flowers, ¾ to 1 inch across, are medium pink with darker pink centers. Slight fragrance. Plants grow 8 to 10 inches tall. Introduced 1962.

PIXIE. Tiny double flowers, less than an inch across, are white with pale pink centers and bloom profusely. Slight fragrance. Plants grow 8 to 10 inches tall. Introduced 1940.

PIXIE GOLD. Medium yellow, semidouble flowers, 1 to 1½ inches across, have 10 to 12 petals each. Slight fragrance. Plants grow 8 to 10 inches tall and are relatively tender. Introduced 1961.

PIXIE ROSE. Medium pink double flowers, ¾ to 1 inch across, bloom in clusters. No fragrance. Plants grow 8 to 10 inches tall and are relatively tender. Introduced 1961.

RED IMP (also called Maid Marion and Mon Tresor). Double flowers, ¾ to 1 inch across, are deep crimson and have a slight fragrance. Plants grow as tiny upright bushes, 8 to 9 inches tall, with few thorns. Introduced 1951.

ROBIN. Double flowers of 60 to 70 petals each, 1 to 1¼ inches across, are rich red and bloom in clusters of up to 15. No fragrance. Plants grow 10 to 12 inches tall. Introduced 1956.

ROULETII. Tiny double flowers, less than ½ inch across, are light pink and have an unusually long blooming season. Slight fragrance. A hardy, vigorous plant that grows 6 to 8 inches tall, Rouletii has long been popular as a potted house plant and is a parent of many modern miniature roses. Introduced 1933.

SCARLET GEM (also called Scarlet Pimpernel). Double flowers, ¾ to 1 inch across, are orange scarlet and look like small hybrid teas. Slight fragrance. Plants grow 12 to 15 inches tall. Introduced 1961.

STARINA. Well-shaped double flowers are 1½ to 2 inches across, unusually large for a miniature, and orange scarlet in color. No fragrance. Plants grow 15 to 18 inches tall and are relatively tender. Introduced 1965.

SWEET FAIRY. Double flowers, ¾ to 1 inch across, are apple-blossom pink and bloom profusely. Strong fragrance. Plants grow 6 to 8 inches tall. Introduced 1946.

TINKER BELL. Bright pink double flowers, 1 to 1½ inches across, have 55 to 65 petals each. No fragrance. Plants grow 8 to 10 inches tall. Introduced 1954.

TOY CLOWN. Flat, semidouble flowers, ¾ to 1 inch across with less than 20 petals each, are white with red petal edges. No fragrance. Plants have few thorns and grow 15 to 18 inches tall. Introduced 1966.

TWINKLES. White double flowers, 1 to 1¼ inches across, open from flesh pink buds. Moderate fragrance. Plants grow 8 to 10 inches tall and bloom profusely. Introduced 1954.

OPAL JEWEL   ROULETII

SWEET FAIRY

145

Characteristics of 344 roses

	BLOSSOM COLOR*						BLOSSOM SIZE			BLOSSOM TYPE			FRAG-RANCE		PLANT HEIGHT				BLOOMING SEASONS			USES		
	White	Pink	Yellow	Red	Lavender-purple	Multicolor	Under 2 inches	2 to 4 inches	Over 4 inches	Single	Semidouble	Double	Slight to moderate	Strong	Under 2 feet	2 to 4 feet	4 to 6 feet	Over 6 feet	Spring	Fall	Continuous	Beds and borders	Hedges and screens	Fences and trellises
ADELINE (cabbage rose)		●						●				●	●			●			●			●	●	
AGNES (shrub rose)			●					●		●		●	●			●			●	●		●	●	
ALASKA CENTENNIAL (grandiflora)				●					●		●	●				●			●	●		●		
ALFRED DE DALMAS (moss rose)		●						●			●	●	●			●			●	●		●		
ALLEGRO (hybrid tea)				●				●				●	●			●			●		●	●		
AMERICAN BEAUTY (hybrid perpetual)		●						●				●		●		●			●		●	●	●	
AMERICAN HERITAGE (hybrid tea)		●						●				●				●			●		●	●		
AMERICAN PILLAR (large-flowered climber)						●	●	●		●								●	●					●
AMY ROBSART (sweetbrier)		●						●		●		●						●	●			●	●	●
ANGEL FACE (floribunda)					●			●				●	●	●		●			●		●	●	●	
ANNI WELTER (moss rose)		●						●			●	●	●			●			●		●	●		
APOTHECARY ROSE (French rose)			●					●		●				●		●			●		●	●		
APRICOT NECTAR (grandiflora)		●						●			●		●			●			●			●		
AQUARIUS (grandiflora)		●							●		●	●				●			●		●	●		
ARRILLAGA (hybrid perpetual)		●						●			●	●					●	●	●			●		
BABY BETSY McCALL (miniature)		●					●				●	●		●	●				●		●	●		
BABY DARLING (miniature)		●					●				●	●		●	●				●		●	●		
BABY GOLD STAR (miniature)			●				●			●		●		●	●				●		●	●		
BABY MASQUERADE (miniature)					●	●	●				●	●		●	●				●		●	●		
BARON GIROD DE L'AIN (hybrid perpetual)				●				●			●	●		●		●			●	●		●	●	
BARONNE PRÉVOST (hybrid perpetual)		●						●			●	●				●			●	●		●	●	
BEAUTY SECRET (miniature)			●				●				●	●	●	●	●				●		●	●		
BELINDA (hybrid musk)		●						●		●		●				●			●		●	●	●	
BELLE AMOUR (alba rose)		●						●			●	●				●			●		●	●		
BELLE ISIS (French rose)		●						●			●	●		●		●			●		●	●		
BETTY PRIOR (floribunda)		●						●		●		●				●			●		●	●	●	
BEWITCHED (hybrid tea)		●						●			●	●				●			●		●	●		
BISHOP DARLINGTON (hybrid musk)		●						●		●		●					●	●	●		●		●	●
BLACK PRINCE (hybrid perpetual)				●				●			●		●	●		●			●	●		●	●	
BLANC DOUBLE DE COUBERT (shrub rose)	●							●			●	●		●		●			●	●		●	●	
BLANCHEFLEUR (cabbage rose)	●							●				●	●			●			●			●		
BLANCHE MALLERIN (hybrid tea)	●							●				●	●		●				●			●		
BLAZE (large-flowered climber)				●				●		●		●					●	●			●			●
BLOOMFIELD DAINTY (hybrid musk)		●						●		●		●					●		●	●			●	●
BLOSSOMTIME (large-flowered climber)		●						●			●		●				●		●					●
BO-PEEP (miniature)		●					●			●	●		●		●				●		●	●		
BORDER GOLD (floribunda)			●					●			●	●	●			●			●		●	●	●	
BUCCANEER (hybrid tea)			●					●			●	●					●		●		●	●		
BUFF BEAUTY (hybrid musk)			●					●			●	●					●		●	●	●		●	●
CAMAIEUX (French rose)						●		●		●				●		●			●			●		
CAMELOT (grandiflora)		●						●			●	●				●			●		●	●		
CANDY STRIPE (hybrid tea)						●			●		●	●	●	●		●			●		●	●		
CAPITAINE JOHN INGRAM (moss rose)				●				●			●	●		●		●			●		●	●		
CARDINAL DE RICHELIEU (French rose)					●			●			●	●		●			●		●			●	●	
CAROL ANN (polyantha)		●					●				●		●		●				●		●	●		
CARROUSEL (grandiflora)				●				●		●		●				●			●		●	●		
CATHERINE MERMET (tea rose)		●						●			●	●				●			●		●	●		
CÉCILE BRUNNER (polyantha)		●					●	●			●	●				●			●		●	●	●	
CELSIANA (damask rose)		●						●		●			●				●		●			●		
CÉSONIE (damask rose)		●						●			●	●					●		●			●	●	

*Only principal colors are listed. Rose hues vary widely and often change as the flower ages. Some varieties come in more than one color; multicolor covers blends of two or three distinct colors and flowers that are streaked, spotted or heavily tinged with a second or third color.

Variety	White	Pink	Yellow	Red	Lavender-purple	Multicolor	Under 2 inches	2 to 4 inches	Over 4 inches	Single	Semidouble	Double	Slight to moderate	Strong	Under 2 feet	2 to 4 feet	4 to 6 feet	Over 6 feet	Spring	Fall	Continuous	Beds and borders	Hedges and screens	Fences and trellises
CHARLOTTE ARMSTRONG (hybrid tea)				•				•			•	•				•					•	•		
CHERRY GLOW (grandiflora)				•				•			•	•	•			•					•	•		
CHEVY CHASE (rambler)				•		•					•	•					•	•	•					•
CHICAGO PEACE (hybrid tea)						•			•		•	•				•					•	•		
CHIPPER (miniature)		•					•				•	•	•		•						•	•		
CHLORIS (alba rose)		•						•			•	•					•		•			•	•	
CHRISTIAN DIOR (hybrid tea)				•				•			•	•				•					•	•		
CHRISTOPHER STONE (hybrid tea)				•				•			•	•	•			•					•	•		
CHRYSLER IMPERIAL (hybrid tea)				•				•				•		•		•					•	•		
CINDERELLA (miniature)	•						•				•	•	•		•						•	•		
CIRCUS (floribunda)						•		•			•	•				•					•	•	•	
CLAIR MATIN (large-flowered climber)		•						•		•								•			•			•
CLIMBING CADENZA (large-flowered climber)				•				•			•	•				•	•	•			•			•
CLIMBING CÉCILE BRUNNER (climbing polyantha)		•					•				•	•				•	•	•			•			•
CLIMBING CRIMSON GLORY (climbing hybrid tea)				•				•			•	•		•			•	•			•			•
CLIMBING ETOILE DE HOLLANDE (climbing hybrid tea)				•				•			•	•					•	•			•			•
CLIMBING MME. HENRI GUILLOT (climbing hybrid tea)						•		•			•	•					•	•			•			•
CLIMBING MRS. SAM McGREDY (climbing hybrid tea)						•		•			•	•					•	•			•			•
CLIMBING PEACE (climbing hybrid tea)						•			•		•	•					•	•			•			•
CLIMBING PICTURE (climbing hybrid tea)		•						•			•	•					•	•			•			•
CLIMBING PINKIE (climbing polyantha)		•						•		•						•	•	•			•			•
CLIMBING QUEEN ELIZABETH (climbing grandiflora)		•						•			•	•					•	•			•			•
CLIMBING SHOT SILK (climbing hybrid tea)						•		•			•	•		•			•	•			•			•
CLIMBING SHOW GARDEN (large-flowered climber)			•						•		•	•					•	•			•			•
CLIO (hybrid perpetual)		•						•			•	•	•			•			•		•	•		
COLONIAL WHITE (large-flowered climber)	•							•			•	•					•		•					•
COLOR GIRL (floribunda)						•		•		•			•		•				•	•	•	•		
COMANCHE (grandiflora)				•				•			•	•				•					•	•		
COMMANDANT BEAUREPAIRE (Bourbon rose)						•		•			•	•				•			•	•	•	•		
COMMAND PERFORMANCE (hybrid tea)				•				•			•	•		•		•					•	•		
COMMUNIS (moss rose)		•						•			•	•	•			•			•			•		
COMTESSE DE MURINAIS (moss rose)	•							•			•	•	•			•			•			•		
CONFIDENCE (hybrid tea)		•						•			•	•	•			•					•	•		
CORAL DAWN (large-flowered climber)		•							•		•	•					•				•			•
CORALITA (large-flowered climber)		•						•			•	•									•			•
CORAL SATIN (large-flowered climber)		•						•			•	•									•			•
CRAMOISI FONCÉ VELOUTÉ (moss rose)				•				•			•	•				•			•	•		•		
CRESTED MOSS (moss rose)		•						•			•	•				•			•	•		•		
CRIMSON GLORY (hybrid tea)				•				•				•		•		•					•	•		
DAGMAR SPÄTH (floribunda)	•							•		•						•					•	•		
DAINTY BESS (hybrid tea)		•						•		•			•			•					•	•		
DAMASK ROSE (damask rose)		•						•			•	•	•				•		•			•		
DAVE DAVIS (hybrid tea)				•					•		•	•				•					•	•		
DÉSIRÉE PARMENTIER (French rose)		•						•			•	•				•			•			•		
DEUIL DE PAUL FONTAINE (moss rose)				•				•			•	•				•			•	•		•		
DICK KOSTER FULGENS (polyantha)				•			•				•	•			•				•	•	•	•		
DON JUAN (large-flowered climber)				•					•		•	•		•			•				•			•
DORTMUND (Kordesii)				•					•	•							•				•			•
DOUBLOONS (large-flowered climber)			•					•			•	•				•	•	•			•			•
DR. BROWNELL (hybrid tea)			•						•		•	•		•		•					•	•		

	White	Pink	Yellow	Red	Lavender-purple	Multicolor	Under 2 inches	2 to 4 inches	Over 4 inches	Single	Semidouble	Double	Slight to moderate	Strong	Under 2 feet	2 to 4 feet	4 to 6 feet	Over 6 feet	Spring	Fall	Continuous	Beds and borders	Hedges and screens	Fences and trellises
DREAM DUST (floribunda)		●					●				●	●			●						●	●	●	
DR. J. H. NICOLAS (large-flowered climber)		●						●			●	●					●				●			●
DR. W. VAN FLEET (large-flowered climber)		●						●			●	●					●	●			●			●
DUC DE GUICHE (French rose)					●			●			●	●				●		●				●	●	
DUCHESSE DE BRABANT (tea rose)		●						●				●	●		●						●	●	●	
DUET (grandiflora)		●						●			●	●			●						●	●	●	
DWARFKING (miniature)				●			●				●	●		●	●						●	●		
ECLIPSE (hybrid tea)			●					●			●	●			●						●	●		
EL CAPITAN (grandiflora)				●				●			●	●				●					●	●		
ELIZABETH OF GLAMIS (floribunda)		●						●			●	●	●		●						●	●	●	
ELSE POULSEN (floribunda)		●					●			●		●			●						●	●	●	
ERFURT (hybrid musk)				●			●			●			●			●	●	●				●	●	
ETERNAL FLAME (large-flowered climber)		●						●			●		●			●	●	●						
ETOILE DE HOLLANDE (hybrid tea)				●				●			●		●		●						●	●		
EUROPEANA (floribunda)				●				●			●	●			●						●	●		
EUTIN (floribunda)				●				●			●	●			●						●	●		
FANTIN-LATOUR (cabbage rose)		●						●			●	●				●	●				●	●		
FASHION (floribunda)		●						●			●	●			●						●	●	●	
FERDINAND PICHARD (hybrid perpetual)					●			●			●					●	●	●				●		
FIRE KING (floribunda)				●			●				●	●			●						●	●		
FIRST PRIZE (hybrid tea)		●							●		●	●			●						●	●		
FLORADORA (floribunda)				●			●				●	●			●						●	●	●	
FLORA McIVOR (sweetbrier)					●	●			●			●			●	●						●	●	
FRAGRANT CLOUD (hybrid tea)				●					●		●		●		●						●	●		
FRAU DAGMAR HARTOPP (shrub rose)		●					●		●			●		●	●						●	●	●	
FRAU KARL DRUSCHKI (hybrid perpetual)	●							●			●					●					●	●	●	
FRENSHAM (floribunda)				●				●		●		●			●						●	●	●	
FRÜHLINGSGOLD (shrub rose)		●						●	●			●					●	●			●	●		
FRÜHLINGSMORGEN (shrub rose)					●		●	●			●					●	●	●			●	●		
GARDEN PARTY (hybrid tea)	●								●		●	●			●						●	●		
GARNETTE (floribunda)				●			●				●	●			●						●	●		
GAY PRINCESS (grandiflora)		●						●			●	●			●						●	●		
GÉANT DES BATAILLES (hybrid perpetual)				●				●			●	●				●					●	●	●	
GENE BOERNER (floribunda)		●						●			●	●			●						●	●		
GÉNÉRAL JACQUEMINOT (hybrid perpetual)				●				●			●		●			●			●	●	●			
GEORG ARENDS (hybrid perpetual)		●							●		●		●			●					●	●		
GLADIATOR (large-flowered climber)				●					●		●						●				●			●
GLOIRE DE GUILAN (damask rose)		●						●			●		●	●		●					●	●		
GLOIRE DES MOUSSEUX (moss rose)		●						●			●	●				●					●	●		
GOLD CUP (floribunda)			●					●			●	●			●						●	●		
GOLDEN CORONET (floribunda)			●					●			●	●			●						●	●		
GOLDEN GIRL (grandiflora)			●					●			●	●			●						●	●		
GOLDEN MOSS (moss rose)			●					●			●	●				●	●				●			
GOLDEN PRINCE (hybrid tea)			●					●			●	●		●							●	●		
GOLDEN SHOWERS (large-flowered climber)			●					●			●	●				●					●			●
GOLDEN WINGS (shrub rose)			●				●	●		●					●		●	●			●	●		
GOLDILOCKS (floribunda)			●					●			●	●	●			●					●	●		
GOVERNOR MARK HATFIELD (grandiflora)				●				●			●	●				●					●	●		
GRANADA (grandiflora)					●			●			●	●		●							●	●		
GRANDMASTER (hybrid musk)		●						●		●			●			●	●				●	●	●	

Only principal colors are listed. Rose hues vary widely and often change as the flower ages. Some varieties come in more than one color; multicolor covers blends of two or three distinct colors and flowers that are streaked, spotted or heavily tinged with a second or third color.

	BLOSSOM COLOR *						BLOSSOM SIZE			BLOSSOM TYPE			FRAGRANCE		PLANT HEIGHT				BLOOMING SEASONS			USES		
	White	Pink	Yellow	Red	Lavender-purple	Multicolor	Under 2 inches	2 to 4 inches	Over 4 inches	Single	Semidouble	Double	Slight to moderate	Strong	Under 2 feet	2 to 4 feet	4 to 6 feet	Over 6 feet	Spring	Fall	Continuous	Beds and borders	Hedges and screens	Fences and trellises
GREAT MAIDEN'S BLUSH (alba rose)		•						•			•	•				•			•			•	•	
GREEN ROSE (China rose)						•		•				•		•		•					•	•		
GROOTENDORST SUPREME (shrub rose)				•		•		•				•				•	•		•		•	•	•	
HANSA (shrub rose)				•		•			•			•	•			•			•		•	•	•	
HAPPY (polyantha)				•			•					•	•						•	•	•	•	•	
HARISON'S YELLOW (shrub rose)			•			•			•			•		•			•	•			•	•	•	
HAWAII (hybrid tea)				•				•			•	•		•		•					•	•		
HECTOR DEANE (grandiflora)				•			•				•	•		•		•					•	•		
HENRI MARTIN (moss rose)				•			•		•			•				•		•		•		•	•	
HENRY NEVARD (hybrid perpetual)				•				•			•	•		•		•	•				•	•		
HERMOSA (China rose)		•					•				•	•			•						•	•		
HUGH DICKSON (hybrid perpetual)				•			•				•	•		•		•	•	•				•	•	
ICEBERG (floribunda)	•						•				•	•				•					•	•	•	
ICE WHITE (floribunda)	•						•				•	•	•			•					•	•	•	
INDIAN GOLD (floribunda)						•		•			•	•				•					•	•	•	
IRISH MIST (floribunda)			•				•				•	•				•					•	•	•	
IVORY FASHION (floribunda)	•						•			•	•	•				•					•	•	•	
JANTZEN GIRL (grandiflora)				•				•			•	•			•						•	•		
JEANNE D'ARC (alba rose)		•					•					•				•			•			•	•	
JIMINY CRICKET (floribunda)						•	•				•	•				•					•	•	•	
JOHN HOPPER (hybrid perpetual)		•						•			•	•	•			•			•	•		•	•	
JOHN S. ARMSTRONG (grandiflora)				•			•				•	•				•					•	•		
JULES MARGOTTIN (hybrid perpetual)		•					•				•	•				•			•	•		•	•	
JULIE DE MERSENT (moss rose)		•					•				•	•				•					•	•		
JUNE BRIDE (grandiflora)	•						•				•	•				•					•	•		
KATHLEEN (hybrid musk)		•						•		•		•				•	•	•			•	•	•	
KING'S RANSOM (hybrid tea)			•					•			•	•				•					•	•		
KÖNIGIN VON DÄNEMARK (alba rose)		•					•					•	•			•			•			•	•	
KORDES' PERFECTA (hybrid tea)						•		•			•	•	•			•					•	•		
LADY PENZANCE (sweetbrier)		•					•		•			•				•	•	•			•	•	•	
LANEII (moss rose)			•				•				•	•				•		•			•	•		
LAURA (hybrid tea)		•						•			•	•				•					•	•		
LEDA (damask rose)		•					•				•	•				•			•			•	•	
LILAC CHARM (floribunda)					•		•			•			•			•					•	•	•	
LITTLE DARLING (floribunda)					•	•						•	•			•					•	•	•	
LORD PENZANCE (sweetbrier)			•				•		•			•				•	•	•			•	•	•	•
LOUIS GIMARD (moss rose)		•					•					•				•		•			•	•		
LUCKY LADY (grandiflora)		•					•				•	•			•						•	•		
LUCKY PIECE (hybrid tea)						•		•			•	•			•						•	•		
MABELLE STEARNS (shrub rose)		•					•					•		•	•						•	•		
MABEL MORRISON (hybrid perpetual)	•							•			•	•				•			•	•		•	•	
MAMAN COCHET (tea rose)		•					•				•	•			•						•	•		
MARCHIONESS OF LONDONDERRY (hybrid perpetual)		•						•			•	•				•	•	•			•	•		
MARÉCHAL NIEL (noisette rose)			•				•				•	•	•				•	•	•			•		•
MARGO KOSTER (polyantha)		•			•						•	•	•		•						•	•	•	
MATTERHORN (hybrid tea)	•						•				•	•					•				•	•		
MAX GRAF (shrub rose)		•					•	•		•			•		•				•			•		
MIRANDY (hybrid tea)				•				•			•		•		•						•	•		
MISS ALL-AMERICAN BEAUTY (hybrid tea)		•						•			•		•			•					•	•		
MISS FRANCE (grandiflora)				•				•			•	•				•					•	•	•	

149

	Blossom Color*						Blossom Size			Blossom Type			Fragrance		Plant Height				Blooming Seasons			Uses		
	White	Pink	Yellow	Red	Lavender-purple	Multicolor	Under 2 inches	2 to 4 inches	Over 4 inches	Single	Semidouble	Double	Slight to moderate	Strong	Under 2 feet	2 to 4 feet	4 to 6 feet	Over 6 feet	Spring	Fall	Continuous	Beds and borders	Hedges and screens	Fences and trellises
MISTER LINCOLN (hybrid tea)				●				●				●	●			●					●	●		
MLLE. FRANZISKA KRÜGER (tea rose)					●			●			●	●		●							●	●		
MME. ERNST CALVAT (Bourbon rose)		●						●			●	●		●		●	●	●			●			●
MME. GRÉGOIRE STAECHELIN (large-flowered climber)		●						●		●		●		●			●	●			●			●
MME. HARDY (damask rose)	●							●			●	●	●			●	●				●	●		
MME. LEGRAS DE ST. GERMAIN (alba rose)	●							●			●	●				●	●				●	●		
MME. LOUIS LÉVÊQUE (moss rose)		●						●			●	●	●			●	●	●			●	●		
MME. PIERRE OGER (Bourbon rose)						●		●			●	●	●			●	●			●	●	●		
MOJAVE (hybrid tea)				●				●			●	●		●						●	●		
MONTEZUMA (grandiflora)				●				●			●	●		●						●	●		
MOTHERSDAY (polyantha)				●				●			●	●		●						●	●		
MOUNTAIN HAZE (floribunda)					●			●			●	●	●							●	●		
MOUNT SHASTA (grandiflora)	●								●		●	●				●				●	●		
MRS. ARTHUR CURTISS JAMES (large-flowered climber)			●						●	●			●				●	●			●			
MRS. DUDLEY CROSS (tea rose)			●					●			●	●		●						●	●		
MRS. JOHN LAING (hybrid perpetual)		●						●				●	●			●				●	●		
NEVADA (shrub rose)	●							●	●							●	●	●			●		
NEW DAWN (large-flowered climber)		●						●			●	●					●			●			●
NUITS DE YOUNG (moss rose)				●			●				●			●			●			●	●		
OAKINGTON RUBY (miniature)				●			●				●		●							●	●		
OKLAHOMA (hybrid tea)				●					●		●		●		●					●	●		
OLD BLUSH (China rose)		●						●		●		●	●			●				●	●		
OLÉ (grandiflora)				●				●			●	●	●			●				●	●		
OMAR KHAYYAM (damask rose)		●						●			●	●		●			●			●	●		
OPAL JEWEL (miniature)		●					●				●	●	●							●	●		
ORANGE CHIFFON (floribunda)			●					●		●				●						●	●	●	
ORANGE TRIUMPH (polyantha)				●			●			●		●		●						●	●	●	
PARKDIREKTOR RIGGERS (Kordesii)				●			●			●		●				●				●	●		●
PARKJUWEL (cabbage rose)		●						●			●		●		●				●		●	●		
PASCALI (hybrid tea)	●							●			●	●			●					●	●		
PAUL NEYRON (hybrid perpetual)		●							●		●	●			●				●	●	●		
PAUL'S SCARLET CLIMBER (large-flowered climber)				●				●		●		●					●	●			●		●
PEACE (hybrid tea)			●						●		●	●			●					●	●		
PETITE DE HOLLANDE (cabbage rose)		●						●			●	●	●			●				●			
PHARAOH (hybrid tea)				●					●		●	●	●							●	●		
PILLAR OF FIRE (climbing floribunda)				●			●				●	●				●				●	●		●
PINK BOUNTIFUL (floribunda)		●							●		●	●	●							●	●	●	
PINK CAMEO (climbing miniature)		●					●				●	●	●							●			●
PINK GROOTENDORST (shrub rose)		●					●			●		●				●	●			●	●		
PINK PARFAIT (grandiflora)		●						●			●	●			●					●	●		
PINOCCHIO (floribunda)		●					●			●		●		●					●	●	●	●	
PIXIE (miniature)	●						●				●	●	●							●	●		
PIXIE GOLD (miniature)			●				●			●		●	●							●	●		
PIXIE ROSE (miniature)		●					●				●	●	●							●	●		
POULSEN'S PARK ROSE (shrub rose)		●							●		●			●						●	●	●	
PRAIRIE DAWN (shrub rose)		●						●			●			●		●	●			●	●		
PRAIRIE FIRE (shrub rose)				●				●			●	●		●						●	●		
PRIDE OF NEWARK (floribunda)		●						●			●	●	●							●	●		
PRINCE CAMILLE DE ROHAN (hybrid perpetual)				●				●			●	●	●			●	●			●	●		
PROLIFERA DE REDOUTÉ (cabbage rose)		●						●			●	●			●		●			●	●		

Only principal colors are listed. Rose hues vary widely and often change as the flower ages. Some varieties come in more than one color; multicolor covers blends of two or three distinct colors and flowers that are streaked, spotted or heavily tinged with a second or third color.

	BLOSSOM COLOR *						BLOSSOM SIZE			BLOSSOM TYPE			FRA-GRANCE		PLANT HEIGHT				BLOOMING SEASONS			USES		
	White	Pink	Yellow	Red	Lavender-purple	Multicolor	Under 2 inches	2 to 4 inches	Over 4 inches	Single	Semidouble	Double	Slight to moderate	Strong	Under 2 feet	2 to 4 feet	4 to 6 feet	Over 6 feet	Spring	Fall	Continuous	Beds and borders	Hedges and screens	Fences and trellises
PROSPERITY (hybrid musk)	●							●			●		●			●	●				●		●	●
QUEEN ELIZABETH (grandiflora)		●						●			●	●					●				●	●	●	
QUEEN OF BERMUDA (grandiflora)			●					●				●	●			●					●	●		
RED EMPRESS (large-flowered climber)			●						●			●	●				●				●			●
RED GLORY (floribunda)			●					●			●			●		●					●	●	●	
REDGOLD (floribunda)				●				●			●	●		●							●	●	●	
RED IMP (miniature)			●				●				●	●		●							●	●		
RED PINOCCHIO (floribunda)			●					●			●	●		●							●	●	●	
RED PROVENCE (cabbage rose)			●					●			●		●		●				●		●	●		
REINE DES VIOLETTES (hybrid perpetual)					●			●			●		●			●	●	●			●			
REINE VICTORIA (Bourbon rose)		●				●					●	●		●							●	●		
RHODE ISLAND RED (large-flowered climber)			●						●		●	●				●	●	●						●
RHONDA (large-flowered climber)		●						●			●	●					●			●				●
RITTER VON BARMSTEDE (Kordesii)		●					●			●						●			●					●
ROBIN (miniature)			●				●				●			●						●	●			
ROBIN HOOD (shrub rose)		●					●			●					●		●	●		●	●			
ROMAN HOLIDAY (floribunda)				●			●				●	●		●						●	●	●		
ROSA ALBA (alba rose)	●						●		●	●	●	●				●	●			●				
ROSA CENTIFOLIA (cabbage rose)		●						●			●	●			●		●			●				
ROSA CENTIFOLIA BULLATA (cabbage rose)		●						●			●		●			●				●				
ROSA EGLANTERIA (sweetbrier)		●					●		●							●		●			●	●		
ROSA FOETIDA BICOLOR (shrub rose)				●			●		●				●			●		●				●		
ROSA FOETIDA PERSIANA (shrub rose)			●					●			●					●		●				●		
ROSA HUGONIS (shrub rose)			●					●		●						●	●			●				
ROSALEEN (hybrid musk)			●					●			●					●	●	●		●	●			
ROSA MOYESII (shrub rose)			●				●		●							●	●			●			●	
ROSA MUNDI (French rose)				●			●			●	●					●			●					
ROSA RUBRIFOLIA (shrub rose)		●					●		●							●	●			●				
ROSA RUGOSA (shrub rose)			●					●		●		●				●	●			●	●		●	
ROSA RUGOSA ALBA (shrub rose)	●							●		●		●				●	●			●	●		●	
ROSE À PARFUM DE L'HAY (shrub rose)			●					●			●		●			●	●			●	●		●	
ROSE DE MEAUX (cabbage rose)		●				●				●			●	●	●		●			●				
ROSE DES PEINTRES (cabbage rose)		●						●			●	●			●	●			●		●	●		
ROSE DES QUATRE SAISONS (damask rose)		●						●			●	●		●				●	●	●				
ROSE DU ROI (damask rose)			●					●		●			●		●		●	●		●	●			
ROSENELFE (floribunda)		●					●			●	●		●							●	●	●		
ROULETII (miniature)		●					●			●	●		●							●	●			
ROUNDELAY (grandiflora)			●					●			●	●		●						●	●			
ROYAL HIGHNESS (hybrid tea)		●						●			●	●	●		●					●	●			
RUHM VON STEINFURTH (hybrid perpetual)			●				●				●	●			●	●	●			●	●			
RUMBA (floribunda)				●	●		●				●	●		●						●	●	●		
SAFRANO (tea rose)			●				●			●		●		●						●	●			
SALET (moss rose)		●					●				●		●		●				●	●	●			
SAN ANTONIO (grandiflora)			●					●			●				●					●	●			
SARAH VAN FLEET (shrub rose)		●						●	●		●				●			●	●	●	●	●		
SARATOGA (floribunda)	●						●			●		●	●						●	●	●			
SCARLET GEM (miniature)			●		●			●			●	●	●							●	●			
SCARLET KNIGHT (grandiflora)			●				●		●		●	●				●				●	●			
SCHNEEZWERG (shrub rose)	●					●			●					●			●		●	●	●	●		
SOMBREUIL (tea rose)	●							●			●		●				●			●				●

	Blossom Color*						Blossom Size			Blossom Type			Fragrance		Plant Height				Blooming Seasons			Uses		
	White	Pink	Yellow	Red	Lavender-purple	Multicolor	Under 2 inches	2 to 4 inches	Over 4 inches	Single	Semidouble	Double	Slight to moderate	Strong	Under 2 feet	2 to 4 feet	4 to 6 feet	Over 6 feet	Spring	Fall	Continuous	Beds and borders	Hedges and screens	Fences and trellises
SOUVENIR DE LA MALMAISON (Bourbon rose)		●						●				●	●			●					●	●	●	
SOUVENIR DE MME. H. THURET (hybrid perpetual)				●				●				●	●			●					●	●	●	●
SNOW WHITE (polyantha)	●					●						●		●							●	●	●	●
SPARRIESHOOP (shrub rose)		●					●		●			●				●	●	●				●		
SPARTAN (floribunda)				●			●					●	●		●						●	●	●	
SPECTACULAR (large-flowered climber)				●			●				●	●				●				●				●
STADT ROSENHEIM (shrub rose)				●			●				●	●					●		●				●	●
STARFIRE (grandiflora)				●				●				●	●			●				●	●			
STARINA (miniature)				●				●			●			●						●	●			
STRAWBERRY BLONDE (grandiflora)				●			●					●	●			●				●	●			
SUNSPOT (floribunda)			●					●			●					●				●	●	●		
SUTTER'S GOLD (hybrid tea)			●					●			●		●			●				●	●			
SWARTHMORE (hybrid tea)		●						●			●	●					●			●	●			
SWEET AND LOW (floribunda)		●				●				●	●		●							●	●	●		
SWEET FAIRY (miniature)		●				●				●	●	●	●							●	●			
THE FAIRY (polyantha)		●				●				●			●							●	●	●		
THÉRÈSE BUGNET (shrub rose)		●				●				●	●			●		●				●	●	●		
TIFFANY (hybrid tea)					●			●			●	●	●			●				●	●			
TINKER BELL (miniature)		●				●				●			●							●	●			
TOY CLOWN (miniature)					●	●			●			●								●	●			
TROJAN (grandiflora)					●			●			●	●			●					●	●			
TROPICANA (hybrid tea)				●				●			●		●		●					●	●			
TUSCANY (French rose)				●			●		●		●			●			●			●	●			
TWINKLES (miniature)	●					●				●	●	●								●	●			
VARIEGATA DI BOLOGNA (Bourbon rose)					●	●			●		●			●	●	●					●	●	
VIERGE DE CLÉRY (cabbage rose)	●						●				●	●			●	●				●	●	
VIKING QUEEN (large-flowered climber)		●					●				●	●				●			●				●
VIOLACÉE (moss rose)					●		●				●					●				●	●			
VOGUE (floribunda)		●					●				●	●			●					●	●	●		
WALDFEE (hybrid perpetual)				●			●				●	●				●	●	●		●	●		
WHITE BATH (moss rose)	●						●				●	●	●		●		●			●	●		
WHITE DAWN (large-flowered climber)	●						●				●	●				●			●				●
WHITE KNIGHT (hybrid tea)	●						●					●			●					●	●			
WHITE MAMAN COCHET (tea rose)	●						●				●	●			●					●	●			
WHITE WINGS (hybrid tea)	●						●		●	●			●		●					●	●			
WILLIAM LOBB (moss rose)				●			●		●		●						●	●					●
WILLIAM R. SMITH (tea rose)				●			●				●	●		●						●	●			
WILL SCARLET (hybrid musk)				●			●		●		●					●			●		●	●
WITCHING HOUR (floribunda)				●			●			●			●			●				●	●	●		
WORLD'S FAIR (floribunda)				●			●			●		●	●			●				●	●	●		
YORK AND LANCASTER (damask rose)					●	●			●		●			●			●		●		●	●		
ZÉPHIRINE DROUHIN (Bourbon rose)		●					●				●	●				●	●	●			●	●
ZEUS (large-flowered climber)			●				●			●	●					●			●				●
ZWEIBRÜCKEN (Kordesii)				●			●				●	●				●			●				●

Only principal colors are listed. Rose hues vary widely and often change as the flower ages. Some varieties come in more than one color; multicolor covers blends of two or three distinct colors and flowers that are streaked, spotted or heavily tinged with a second or third color.

AVERAGE MINIMUM
WINTER TEMPERATURE

Zones 1 and 2,
below −40°

Zones 3, 4 and 5,
−10° to −40°

Zones 6 and 7, 10°
to −10°

Zones 8, 9 and 10,
40° to 10°

How climate affects rose growing

The kinds of roses that summer can bring depend more than anything else on conditions when there are no roses—particularly on the depth of winter cold in the garden.

A guide to the influence of climate is provided by the map above, a simplified version of the U.S. Department of Agriculture climate map that divides North America into 10 zones according to average minimum winter temperature. Here the 10 zones are grouped into four color bands representing areas with distinctive rose-growing requirements. They are referred to in the text of this book by their zone numbers, and indicate what classes of roses you can grow successfully in your locality

(Chapter 4), when you should plant, prune and feed them and what kind of winter protection you should give them *(Chapter 2).*

Many of the older types of roses, notably the polyanthas and the hybrid perpetuals, are especially cold resistant—hardy—and are recommended for areas where winters are severe. However, all of the modern hybrid roses described in this book —the hybrid teas, floribundas and grandifloras —can be grown over most of North America if given the proper type of winter protection—the exception being central Canada, the lightest red band on the map, where the average minimum winter temperature reaches 40° and more below zero.

Picture Credits

The sources for the illustrations that appear in this book are listed below. Credits for pictures from left to right are separated by semicolons, from top to bottom by dashes. Cover—Robert Walch. 4—Keith Martin courtesy James Underwood Crockett; Leonard Wolfe. 6—Robert Walch. 10 through 20—Drawings by Vincent Lewis. 23,24—Nicholas Foster. 25—Nicholas Foster except top right Clarence A. Blaine. 26 through 29—Nicholas Foster. 30,31—Nicholas Foster; Robert Walch. 32,33—Bill Atkinson. 34—Nicholas Foster (2)—Bill Atkinson. 35—Robert Walch. 36,37—Nicholas Foster. 38,39—Bill Atkinson. 40,41—Robert Walch. 42—Nicholas Foster. 44 through 70—Drawings by Vincent Lewis except pages 54 and 56 drawings by Sy and Dorothea Barlowe. 73—Frank Lerner courtesy The Free Library of Philadelphia. 74,75—Henry B. Beville courtesy Smithsonian Institution; Lee Boltin courtesy The Chase Manhattan Bank Money Museum, N.Y.—Hannibal courtesy Archeological Museum, Herakleion. 76,77—David Lees courtesy Palazzo Pubblico, Siena; Hallmark Gallery courtesy Worcester Art Museum; Giraudon courtesy Cathédrale Notre-Dame de Paris. 78—The American Numismatic Society, N.Y.—Lee Boltin courtesy Jean Gordon—Lee Boltin courtesy The Chase Manhattan Bank Money Museum, N.Y. 79—Lee Boltin courtesy The Chase Manhattan Bank Money Museum, N.Y. (2)—Lee Boltin courtesy Jean Gordon (2); Lee Boltin courtesy Private Collection—Lee Boltin courtesy Private Collection. 80—The Metropolitan Museum of Art, gift of J. Pierpont Morgan, 1911—The Metropolitan Museum of Art, Munsey Fund, 1932. 81—F. W. Smith painted by D. S. Hopkinson—Howard C. Moore (Woodmansterne Ltd.) courtesy Winchester Castle—Courtesy Ghent University Library. 82—Pierre Boulat courtesy Musée National de Malmaison. 83—Pierre Boulat courtesy Bibliothèque Nationale, Paris. 84—Robert Walch. 89 through 97—Drawings by Vincent Lewis. 99 through 105—Pedro Guerrero. 106 through 145—Illustrations by Allianora Rosse. 153—Map by Adolphe E. Brotman.

Acknowledgments

For their help in the preparation of this book, the editors wish to thank the following: Mrs. Paul Abbott, Southampton, N.Y.; Matthew A. R. Bassity, New York City; F. Raymond Brush, Executive Secretary, American Association of Nurserymen, Washington, D.C.; David Carson, Horticulturist, Nantucket, Mass.; Mrs. Edith Crockett, Librarian, Horticultural Society of New York, New York City; Mrs. Jane E. Foster, Copy, Media and Public Relations Director, Jackson and Perkins Co., Medford, Ore.; Harold S. Goldstein, Executive Secretary, Editor, American Rose Society, Columbus, Ohio; Mrs. Jean Gordon, Ocean Grove, N.J.; George Greene, Curator of Old Roses, Missouri Botanical Garden, St. Louis, Mo.; Miss Elizabeth Hall, Senior Librarian, Horticultural Society of New York, New York City; Richard V. Hare, New York City; P. A. Haring, Stony Brook, N.Y.; Tom Huston, President, Huston Research Corporation, Miami, Fla.; Richard J. Hutton, Treasurer, Star Roses, West Grove, Pa.; Karl P. Jones, Barrington, R.I.; George A. Kalmbacher, Plant Taxonomist, Brooklyn Botanic Garden, N.Y.; Dr. Eldon W. Lyle, Plant Pathologist, Texas Rose Research Foundation, Tyler, Texas; John P. Meszaros, Director, Hershey Rose Garden and Arboretum, Hershey, Pa.; James C. Risk, Coin Galleries, New York City; George Rose, Director of Public Relations, Secretary and Treasurer, All-America Rose Selections, Shenandoah, Iowa; Mr. and Mrs. Alfred Saxdel, Shaw Gardens, St. Louis, Mo.; Mrs. H. Allan Sillcox, Southampton, N.Y.; Miss Nora Smith, Bernardsville, N.J.; Mrs. Patricia Spence, American Rose Society, Columbus, Ohio; Mrs. Dorothy Stemler, Tillotson's Roses, Watsonville, Calif.; Richard Thompson, Wynnewood, Pa.; Mrs. Petrea Tzagournis, Librarian, American Rose Society, Columbus, Ohio; Mrs. Sonia Wedge, Reference Librarian, New York Botanical Garden Library, N.Y.; Thomas M. Yerkes, Secretary, Star Roses, West Grove, Pa. Recipe for rose-petal jam on page 16 courtesy of Hamlyn Publishing Group Ltd., Feltham, Middlesex, England.

Bibliography

ROSES—General

Allen, R. C., *Roses for Every Garden*. M. Barrows and Company, Inc., 1962.

Bassity, Matthew A. R., *The Magic World of Roses*. Hearthside Press, Inc., 1966.

Kiaer, Eigil, *The Concise Handbook of Roses*. E. P. Dutton & Co., Inc., 1966.

McFarland, L.H.D. and Robert Pyle, *How to Grow Roses*. Rev. 3rd ed. The Macmillan Company, 1968.

Modern Roses 7: The International Check-list of Roses. The McFarland Company, 1969.

Rockwell, F. F. and Esther C. Grayson, *The Rockwells' Complete Book of Roses*. Revised and Lists Updated. Doubleday & Company, Inc., 1966.

Thomas, Graham Stuart, *Climbing Roses Old and New*. St. Martin's Press, 1966.

Shrub Roses of Today. Phoenix House Ltd., London, 1962.

Thomson, Richard and Helen Van Pelt Wilson, *Roses for Pleasure*. D. Van Nostrand Company, Inc., 1957.

Westcott, Cynthia, *Anyone Can Grow Roses*. D. Van Nostrand Company, Inc., 1965.

OLD ROSES

Bunyard, Edward A., *Old Garden Roses*. Charles Scribner's Sons, 1937.

Stemler, Dorothy, *The Book of Old Roses*. Bruce Humphries Publishers, 1966.

Thomas, Graham Stuart, *The Old Shrub Roses*. Phoenix House Ltd., London, 1963.

Thomson, Richard, *Old Roses for Modern Gardens*. D. Van Nostrand Company, Inc., 1959.

THE HISTORY OF ROSES

Gordon, Jean, *Pageant of the Rose*. Studio Publications in association with Thomas Y. Crowell Company, 1953.

Seward, Barbara, *The Symbolic Rose*. Columbia University Press, 1960.

Shepherd, Roy E., *History of the Rose*. The Macmillan Company, 1954.

Where to see roses

Among the most popular tourist attractions in North America are some 250 public rose gardens, which draw millions of visitors a year. They are the best places to learn firsthand about the many varieties of roses, and to see newly developed strains, prize winners and rarely grown types. Most of the gardens open in spring and remain open until the plants stop blooming in the fall or early winter. A representative selection of 97 gardens around the United States and Canada is given below.

CALIFORNIA
Arcadia — Arcadia Park
Berkeley — Berkeley Municipal Rose Garden
La Canada — Descanso Gardens
Los Angeles — Exposition Park Rose Garden
Oakland — Morcum Amphitheatre of Roses
Sacramento — Capitol Park Rose Garden
San Francisco — Golden Gate Park Rose Garden
San Jose — San Jose Municipal Rose Garden
Santa Barbara — Santa Barbara Memorial Test Garden
Whittier — Rose Hills Memorial Park

COLORADO
Denver — Denver Botanic Gardens

CONNECTICUT
Norwich — Norwich Memorial Rose Garden
Hartford — Elizabeth Park Rose Garden

D.C.
Washington — Shoreham Hotel Rose Garden

GEORGIA
Atlanta — Piedmont Park

IDAHO
Boise — Julia Davis Park
Caldwell — Caldwell Municipal Rose Garden

ILLINOIS
Chicago — Marquette Park Rose Garden
Highland Park — Gardener's Memorial Garden
Wheaton — Robert R. McCormick Memorial Gardens

INDIANA
Fort Wayne — Lakeside Rose Garden

IOWA
Ames — Iowa State University Rose Garden
Davenport — Vander Veer Park
Des Moines — Greenwood Park Municipal Rose Garden

KANSAS
Topeka — Reinisch Rose and Rose Test Gardens

KENTUCKY
Louisville — Kentucky Memorial Rose Garden

LOUISIANA
Baton Rouge — L.S.U. Rose Test Garden
Many — Hodges Gardens
New Orleans — New Orleans City Park Rose Garden

MICHIGAN
East Lansing — Michigan State University
Lansing — Cooley Gardens

MINNESOTA
Duluth — Duluth Rose Garden
Minneapolis — Minneapolis Municipal Rose Garden

MISSISSIPPI
Jackson — Municipal Rose Garden

MISSOURI
Cape Girardeau — Capaha Park
Kansas City — Municipal Rose Garden
St. Louis — Missouri Botanical Rose Garden
Municipal Rose Garden in Forest Park

MONTANA
Missoula — Missoula Memorial Rose Garden

NEBRASKA
Lincoln — Cornhusker Memorial Rose Garden
Antelope Park
Omaha — Memorial Park Rose Garden

NEVADA
Reno — Reno Municipal Rose Garden

NEW MEXICO
Albuquerque — Prospect Park Rose Garden

NEW YORK
Buffalo — Humboldt Park
Ithaca — Cornell University Rose Garden
Newark — The National Rose Garden

New York — Brooklyn Botanic Garden
Bronx Park
Rochester — Maplewood Park
Syracuse — Thornden Park
Tuxedo — Sterling Forest Gardens

NORTH CAROLINA
Raleigh — Raleigh Municipal Rose Garden

OHIO
Akron — Goodyear Heights Park
Cincinnati — Ault Park Municipal Rose Garden
Columbus — Columbus Park of Roses
Ohio State University Rose Garden
Mentor — Joseph J. Kern Rose Nursery
Melvin E. Wyant Rose Specialist, Inc.
Wooster — Ohio Agricultural Research Center

OKLAHOMA
Muskogee — Honor Heights Park
Norman — Norman Municipal Rose Garden
Oklahoma City — Will Rogers Park
Tulsa — Tulsa Municipal Rose Garden

OREGON
Eugene — Municipal Rose Garden
Portland — International Rose Test Garden

PENNSYLVANIA
Allentown — Gross Memorial Rose Garden
Hershey — Hershey Rose Gardens and Arboretum
Kennett Square — Longwood Gardens
Pittsburgh — Mellon Park Rose Gardens
Pottstown — Pottstown Municipal Rose Garden
Reading — Reading Municipal Rose Garden
University Park — Penn State University Test Garden

SOUTH CAROLINA
Orangeburg — Edisto Rose Garden

TENNESSEE
Chattanooga — Municipal Rose Garden in Warner Park
Memphis — Audubon Park

TEXAS
Dallas — Samuell-Grand Municipal Rose Garden
El Paso — El Paso Municipal Rose Garden
Fort Worth — Fort Worth Botanic Garden
Houston — Herman Park
Tyler — Tyler Municipal Rose Garden

UTAH
Fillmore — Old Capital State Park
Salt Lake City — Salt Lake City Municipal Rose Garden

VIRGINIA
Arlington — Arlington Memorial Rose Garden
Norfolk — Lafayette Park

WASHINGTON
Bellingham — Fairhaven Park Rose Garden
Seattle — Woodland Park Rose Garden
Spokane — Rose Hill Manito Park
Tacoma — Point Defiance Park Rose Garden

WEST VIRGINIA
Huntington — Ritter Park Rose Garden

WISCONSIN
Hales Corners — Boerner Botanical Gardens
Madison — Olbrich Park

CANADA

B.C.
Victoria — The Butchart Gardens Ltd.

ONTARIO
Niagara Falls — Royal Horticultural Gardens
Windsor — Jackson Park Rose Garden

QUEBEC
Montreal — Connaught Park Rose Garden
Montreal Memorial Park

Index

Numerals in italics indicate an illustration of the subject mentioned

x
PRINTED IN U.S.A.